2013 Conference of the North American Chapter of the Association for Computational Linguistics: Human Language Technologies (NAACL HLT 2013)

Student Research Workshop

Atlanta, Georgia, USA
13 June 2013

ISBN: 978-1-62748-839-6

Printed from e-media with permission by:

Curran Associates, Inc.
57 Morehouse Lane
Red Hook, NY 12571

Some format issues inherent in the e-media version may also appear in this print version.

Printed by Curran Associates, Inc. (2013)

For permission requests, please contact the Association for Computational Linguistics
at the address below.

Association for Computational Linguistics
209 N. Eighth Street
Stroudsburg, Pennsylvania 18360

Phone: 1-570-476-8006
Fax: 1-570-476-0860

acl@aclweb.org

Additional copies of this publication are available from:

Curran Associates, Inc.
57 Morehouse Lane
Red Hook, NY 12571 USA
Phone: 845-758-0400
Fax: 845-758-2634
Email: curran@proceedings.com
Web: www.proceedings.com

Introduction

Welcome to the NAACL HLT 2013 Student Research Workshop.

This year, we have two different kinds of paper: research papers and thesis proposals. Thesis proposals are intended for advanced students who have decided on a thesis topic and wish to get feedback on their proposal and broader ideas for their continuing work, while research papers can describe completed work or work in progress with preliminary results.

All the papers will be presented in the main conference poster session, giving the opportunity for students to interact and present their work to a large and diverse audience. In addition, we have a separate session for the student papers on the first day of workshops (after the main conference). During this session, students will present their papers and receive feedback from mentors. The mentors are experienced researchers who will prepare in-depth comments and questions in advance of the presentation. Each accepted paper is assigned a mentor. The separate session is newly introduced this year and differs from recent NAACL student workshops where student talks were during the main conference sessions or the papers were presented as posters only. We expect that the focused workshop will provide a greater opportunity for receive feedback from mentors, and also allow the students to network and socialize with other student participants.

We received 8 thesis proposals and 15 research papers. Out of these we accepted 6 thesis proposals and 7 research papers leading to an acceptance rate of 75% for thesis proposals and 47% for research papers. We thank our dedicated program committee who gave constructive and detailed reviews for the student papers. We also thank the NAACL 2013 organizing committee—Lucy Vanderwende, Hal Daumé III, Katrin Kirchhoff, Priscilla Rassmussen, Matt Post and Colin Cherry.

Student Chairs:

Annie Louis, University of Edinburgh
Richard Socher, Stanford University

Faculty Advisors:

Julia Hockenmaier, University of Illinois at Urbana-Champaign
Eric Ringger, Brigham Young University

Program Committee:

Yukino Baba, University of Tokyo
Emily Bender, University of Washington
Jonathan Berant, Stanford University
Chris Biemann, University of Darmstadt
Yonatan Bisk, University of Illinois at Urbana-Champaign
Jackie Chi Kit Cheung, University of Toronto
Mark Dredze, Johns Hopkins University
Kevin Duh, NAIST
Jacob Eisenstein, Georgia Institute of Technology
Jason Eisner, Johns Hopkins University
Paul Felt, Brigham Young University
Jennifer Gillenwater, University of Pennsylvania
David Hall, University of California, Berkeley
Derrick Higgins, Educational Testing Service
Yuening Hu, University of Maryland, College Park
Kevin Knight, University of Southern California
Philip Koehn, University of Edinburgh
Diane Littman, University of Pittsburgh
Fei Liu, Bosch Research
Yang Liu, University of Texas at Dallas
Bill Lund, Brigham Young University
Rebecca Mason, Brown University
Rada Mihalcea, University of North Texas
Christopher Potts, Stanford University
Vahed Qazvinian, Google
Preethi Raghavan, The Ohio State University
Marta Recasens, Stanford University
Sravana Reddy, Dartmouth University
Chenhao Tan, Cornell University
Kapil Thadani, Columbia University
Scott Yih, Microsoft Research
Qiuye Zhao, University of Pennsylvania

Table of Contents

Workshop Program

Thursday, June 13, 2013

9:00–9:15 Opening remarks

Session 1: Research paper presentations

9:15–9:30 *Critical Reflections on Evaluation Practices in Coreference Resolution*
Gordana Ilic Holen

9:30–9:45 *Reducing Annotation Effort on Unbalanced Corpus based on Cost Matrix*
Wencan Luo, Diane Litman and Joel Chan

9:45–10:00 *A Machine Learning Approach to Automatic Term Extraction using a Rich Feature Set*
Merley Conrado, Thiago Pardo and Solange Rezende

10:00–10:15 *A Rule-based Approach for Karmina Generation*
Franky Franky

10:15–10:30 *From Language to Family and Back: Native Language and Language Family Identification from English Text*
Ariel Stolerman, Aylin Caliskan and Rachel Greenstadt

10:30–11:00 Coffee break

Session 2: Research paper presentations

11:00–11:15 *Ontology Label Translation*
Mihael Arcan and Paul Buitelaar

11:15–11:30 *Reversing Morphological Tokenization in English-to-Arabic SMT*
Mohammad Salameh, Colin Cherry and Grzegorz Kondrak

Thursday, June 13, 2013 (continued)

Session 3: Thesis proposal presentations

11:30–12:00 *Statistical Machine Translation in Low Resource Settings*
Ann Irvine

12:00–12:30 *Large-Scale Paraphrasing for Natural Language Understanding*
Juri Ganitkevitch

12:30–14:00 Lunch

Session 4: Thesis proposal presentations

14:00–14:30 *Domain-Independent Captioning of Domain-Specific Images*
Rebecca Mason

14:30–15:00 *Helpfulness-Guided Review Summarization*
Wenting Xiong

15:00–15:30 *Entrainment in Spoken Dialogue Systems: Adopting, Predicting and Influencing User Behavior*
Rivka Levitan

15:30–16:00 Coffee break

Session 5: Thesis proposal presentation

16:00–16:30 *User Goal Change Model for Spoken Dialog State Tracking*
Yi Ma

16:30–17:30 Panel

Critical Reflections on Evaluation Practices in Coreference Resolution

Gordana Ilić Holen
Department of Informatics
University of Oslo
Norway
gordanil@ifi.uio.no

Abstract

In this paper we revisit the task of quantitative evaluation of coreference resolution systems. We review the most commonly used metrics (MUC, B^3, CEAF and BLANC) on the basis of their evaluation of coreference resolution in five texts from the OntoNotes corpus. We examine both the correlation between the metrics and the degree to which our human judgement of coreference resolution agrees with the metrics. In conclusion we claim that loss of information value is an essential factor, insufficiently adressed in current metrics, in human perception of the degree of success or failure of coreference resolution. We thus conjecture that including a layer of mention information weight could improve both the coreference resolution and its evaluation.

1 Introduction and motivation

Coreference resolution (CR) is the task of linking together multiple expressions of a given entity (Yang et al., 2003). The field has experienced a surge of interest with several shared tasks in recent years: SemEval 2010 (Recasens et al., 2010), CoNLL 2011 (Pradhan et al., 2011) and CoNLL 2012 (Pradhan et al., 2012). However the field has from the very start been riddled with problems related to the scoring and comparison of CR systems. Currently there are five metrics in wider use: MUC (Vilain et al., 1995), B^3 (Bagga and Baldwin, 1998), the two CEAF metrics (Luo, 2005) and BLANC (Recasens and Hovy, 2011). As there is no global agreement on which metrics are the most appropriate, the above-mentioned shared tasks have used a combination of several metrics to evaluate the contenders. Although coreference resolution is a subproblem of natural language understanding, coreference resolution evaluation metrics have predominately been discussed in terms of abstract entities and hypothetical system errors. In our view, it is of utmost importance to observe actual texts and actual system errors.

2 Background: The metrics

In this section, we will present the five metrics in the usual terms of precision, recall and F-score. We follow the predominant practice and use the term *mention* for individual referring expressions, and *entity* for sets of mentions that refer to the same object (Luo et al., 2004). We use the term *key entity (K)* for gold entities, and *response entity (R)* for entities which were produced by the CR system.

2.1 Link-based: MUC and BLANC

The MUC metric (Vilain et al., 1995) is based on comparing the number of links in the key entity ($|K| - 1$) to the number of links missing from the response entity, routinely calculated as the number of partitions of the key entity $|p(K)|$ minus one, so $Recall = \frac{(|K|-1)-(|p(K)|-1)}{|K|-1} = \frac{|K|-|p(K)|}{|K|-1}$. For the whole document, recalls for entities are simply added: $Recall = \frac{\sum |K_i|-|p(K_i)|}{\sum(|K_i|-1)}$ In calculating precision, the case is inverted: The base entity is now the response, and the question posed is how many missing links have to be added to the key partitions to form the response entity.

BLANC (Recasens and Hovy, 2011) is a variant of the Rand index (Rand, 1971) adapted for the task

Proceedings of the NAACL HLT 2013 Student Research Workshop, pages 1–7,
Atlanta, Georgia, 13 June 2013.

of coreference resolution. The BLANC metric makes use of both coreferent and non-coreferent links, correct and incorrect. The final precision, recall and F-score are the average of the P, R and F-score of corresponding coreferential and non-referential values. However, since this is an analysis of isolated entities, there are no non-coreferential links. For that reason, in this paper we only present *coreferential* precision, recall and F-score for this metric: $P_c = \frac{rc}{rc+wc}$, $R_c = \frac{rc}{rc+wn}$ and $F_c = \frac{2P_cR_c}{P_c+R_c}$, where *rc* is the number of correct coreferential links, *wc* the number of incorrect coreferential links, and *wn* is the number of non-coreferential links incorrectly marked as coreferent by the system.

2.2 Entity and mention-based: B^3 and CEAF

B^3 (Bagga and Baldwin, 1998) calculates precision and recall for every mention in the document, and then combines them to an overall precision and recall. Precision of a single mention m_i is the number of correct mentions in the response entity R_i that contains m_i divided by the total number of mentions in R_i. Recall of m_i is again the number of correct mentions in R_i, this time divided by the number of mentions in the key entity K_i that contains mention m_i. The precision and recall for the entire document can be calculated as weighted sums of precision and recall of the individual mentions. The default weight, also used in this experiment is $\frac{1}{n}$, where n is the number of mentions in the document.

CEAF (Luo, 2005) is based on the best alignment of subsets of key and response entities. For any mapping $g \in G_m$ the total similarity $\Phi(g)$ is the sum of all similarities. The best alignment g^* is found by maximizing the sum of similarities $\Phi(g)$ between the key and response entities, while the maximum total similarity is the sum of the best similarities. Precision and recall are defined in terms of the similarity measure $\Phi(g^*)$: $P = \frac{\Phi(g^*)}{\sum_i \phi(R_i,R_i)}$ $R = \frac{\Phi(g^*)}{\sum_i \phi(K_i,K_i)}$.

There are two versions of CEAF with different similarity measures, $\phi_m(K,R) = |K \cap R|$ and $\phi_e(K,R) = \frac{2|K\cap R|}{|K|+|R|}$. ϕ_e is the basis for CEAF$_e$ which shows a measure of correct entities while CEAF$_m$, based on ϕ_m, shows the percentage of correctly resolved mentions.

	MUC	B^3	CEAF$_e$	CEAF$_m$	BLANC	MELA
MUC	–	0.46	0.22	0.47	0.35	0.63
B^3	0.59	–	0.47	0.56	0.42	0.61
CEAF$_e$	0.46	0.59	–	0.51	0.26	0.38
CEAF$_m$	0.57	0.70	0.62	–	0.46	0.60
BLANC	0.57	0.70	0.57	0.68	–	0.35
MELA	0.59	0.73	0.59	0.70	0.70	–

Table 1: Kendall τ rank correlation coefficient for teams participating in CoNLL shared tasks, with CoNLL 2011 in the upper right, CoNLL 2012 in the lower left corner.

3 Correlating CoNLL shared tasks results

To illustrate the complexity of the present evaluation best practices, we have applied the Kendall τ rank correlation coefficient to the ratings the metrics gave coreference resolution systems that competed in the two recent CoNLL shared tasks. The official metrics of the CoNLL shared tasks was MELA (Denis and Baldridge, 2009), a weighted average of MUC, B^3 and CEAF$_e$.

The results for CoNLL 2011 (Table 1) show a rather weak correlation among the metrics going down to as low as 0.22 between CEAF$_e$ and MUC. Somewhat surprisingly, the two link-based metrics, MUC and BLANC, also show a low degree of agreement (0.35), while the mention-based metrics, CEAF$_m$ and B^3, show the highest agreement of all non-composite metrics. However, this agreement is not particularly high either as the two metrics agree on just above the half of all the cases (0.56).

The results for CoNLL 2012 show much higher correlation among the metrics ranging from 0.46 to 0.70. Again CEAF$_m$ and B^3 show the highest correlation, but unlike in 2011 BLANC "joins" this cluster. CEAF$_e$ and MUC are again least correlated, while CEAF$_e$ and BLANC, in 2011 almost independent, show average correlation (0.57) in 2012.

In our view, comparatively low correlations as well as surprising variation from year to year suggests a certain degree of 'fuzziness' in quantitative coreference resolution evaluation. We leave the investigation of variation between the two years for future work.

4 Error analysis

To better understand the functioning of the metrics we have conducted an error analysis on the key/response entity pairs from five short texts from the development corpus of the CoNLL 2011 Shared Task (Pradhan et al., 2011), one text from each of the five represented genres: Broadcast Conversations (BC), Broadcast News (BN), Magazine (MZ), News Wire (NW) and Web Blogs and News Groups (WB). The texts were chosen as randomly as possible, the only constraint being length[1]. The gold standard texts are originally from OntoNotes 4.0, and contain 64 mentions distributed among 21 key entities. The response texts are the output of Stanford's Multi-Pass Sieve Coreference Resolution System (Lee et al., 2011).

4.1 Categorization

Instead of classifying entities according to their score by some of the metrics, or a combination of several of them, as done by the CoNLL shared tasks, we have based the classification on a notion of linguistic common sense – our subjective idea of how humans evaluate the success or failure of CR. We divide key/response entity pairs into four categories:

- Category 1: Perfect match
- Category 2: Partial match
- Category 3: Merged entities
- Category 4: Failed coreference resolution

We will concentrate on the amount of informational value from the key entity that has been preserved in the response entity. In the course of these experiments, our aim is to see if that rather informal idea can be operationalized in a way amenable to future use in automated CR and/or quantitative evaluation.

4.1.1 Category 1: Perfect match

This class consists of four key/response entity pairs with complete string match. The key and response entities being identical, all metrics show unanimously precision and recall of 100%. The informational value is, of course, completely preserved. Unfortunately, those examples are few and simple: They constitute only 19% of the entities and 14% of mentions in this sample, and all seem to be achieved by the simplest form of string matching.

Key entities	Response entities		MUC	B^3	$CEAF_e$	$CEAF_m$	BLANC
BC45							
• The KMT vice chairman • Wang Jin-pyng • his • his • He • he	• Wang Jin-pyng • his • his • He • he	P R F	100.00 80.00 88.89	100.00 83.33 90.91	90.90 90.90 90.90	100.00 83.33 90.91	100.00 66.67 80.00
BC22							
• KMT Chairman Lien Chan • Chairman Lien Chan • Lien Chan	• KMT Chairman Lien Chan • Lien Chan	P R F	100.00 50.00 66.67	100.00 66.67 80.00	80.00 80.00 80.00	100.00 66.67 80.00	100.00 33.33 50.00
BN1							
• Bill Clinton • The President • he • his • Mr.Clinton • his • He • he	• Bill Clinton • Mr.Clinton • his • He • he	P R F	100.00 85.71 92.31	100.00 62.50 76.92	76.92 76.92 76.92	100.00 62.50 76.92	68.42 46.43 55.32
NW2							
• New Zealand • New Zealand • New Zealand • New Zealand's • New • Zealand	• New Zealand • New Zealand • New Zealand • New Zealand's	P R F	100.00 75.00 85.71	100.00 80.00 88.89	88.89 88.89 88.89	100.00 80.00 88.89	100.00 60.00 75.00

Table 2: Category 2a: Partial match (partial entities)

4.1.2 Category 2: Partial match

The partial response entities can be divided in two subcategories: **2a)** The cases where the response *entities* are partial, i.e.they form a proper subset of the key entity mentions (Table 2) and **2b)** The cases where the response *mentions* are partial, i.e. substrings of the corresponding key mentions (Table 3).

The scoring of the examples has followed CoNLL shared tasks' strict mention detection requirements[2] with the consequence that Category 2b entities have received considerably lower scores than the Category 2a entities even in cases where the loss of informational value has been comparable. For instance, the response entity NW1 (Table 3) has received an average F-score of 56.67%, but its loss of informational value is comparable to that in entities BC45 and BN1 (Table 2). The BC45's response entity has lost the information that `Jiyun Tian` is a `vice-chief`, while entities BC45 and BN1 have lost the information that the person referred to

[1]The texts longer than five sentences were discarded, to make the analysis tractable.

[2]Only response mentions with boundaries identical to the gold mentions are recognized as correct (Pradhan et al., 2011)

is `The KMT vice chairman` (BC45) and `The President` (BN1). However, the latter mentions have received a considerably higher average F-score of 88.32% and 75.68% respectively. This indicates that stricter mention detection requirements do not necessarily improve the quality of CR evaluation.

Key entities	Response entities		MUC	B^3	$CEAF_e$	$CEAF_m$	BLANC
MZ22							
• a school in Shenzhen for the children of Hong Kong expats • the school in Shenzhen	• a school in Shenzhen • the school in Shenzhen	P	0.00	50.00	50.00	50.00	0.00
		R	0.00	50.00	50.00	50.00	0.00
		F	0.00	50.00	50.00	50.00	0.00
NW0							
• China's People's Congress • China's People's Congress	• People's Congress • People's Congress	P	0.00	0.00	0.00	0.00	0.00
		R	0.00	0.00	0.00	0.00	0.00
		F	0.00	0.00	0.00	0.00	0.00
NW1							
• vice-chief committee member Jiyun Tian • Jiyun Tian • He	• committee member Jiyun Tian • Jiyun Tian • He	P	50.00	66.67	66.67	66.67	33.33
		R	50.00	66.67	66.67	66.67	33.33
		F	50.00	66.67	66.67	66.67	33.33
NW5							
• China's People's Congress delegation led by vice-chief committee member Jiyun Tian • the delegation from China's People's Congress	• China's People's Congress delegation • the delegation from China's People's Congress	P	0.00	50.00	50.00	50.00	0.00
		R	0.00	50.00	50.00	50.00	0.00
		F	0.00	50.00	50.00	50.00	0.00

Table 3: Category 2b: Partial match (partial mentions).

4.1.3 Category 3: Merged entities

This category consists of response entities that contain mentions from two or more key entities (Table 4). Our sample contains only four examples in this category, but it is still possible to discern two subcategories:

1. The new information is incorrect
In the key entity MZ40, the sex of the gender-neutral `her ten-year-old child` has been given by the mention `him`. Replacing it with the mention `she` in the response entity gives the wrong information about the child's sex. Entities BN2 and MZ17 also belong to this subcategory, but here the mentions in the response entity are morphologically inconsistent, thus making the mistake easier to detect.

2. The new information is correct or neutral
In entity pair MZ19 the key mention `the latter group` was replaced with response mention `them`,

Key entities	Response entities		MUC	B^3	$CEAF_e$	$CEAF_m$	blanc
BN2							
• he and his wife, now a New York senator • their	• The President • he and his wife, now a New York senator • he • his	P	66.67	25.00	33.33	25.00	0.00
		R	0.00	50.00	33.33	50.00	0.00
		F	0.00	33.33	33.33	33.33	0.00
MZ19							
• the more affluent Taiwanese • their • the latter group	• the more affluent Taiwanese • their • them	P	50.00	66.67	66.67	66.67	33.33
		R	50.00	66.67	66.67	66.67	33.33
		F	50.00	66.67	66.67	66.67	33.33
MZ17							
• her elder son and daughter • them	• her elder son and daughter • him • him	P	0.00	33.33	40.00	33.33	0.00
		R	0.00	50.00	40.00	50.00	0.00
		F	0.00	40.00	40.00	40.00	0.00
MZ40							
• Her ten-year-old child • him • The child • him	• Her ten-year-old child • she • The child	P	50.00	66.67	57.14	66.67	33.33
		R	33.33	50.00	57.14	50.00	20.00
		F	40.00	57.14	57.14	57.14	25.00

Table 4: Category 3: Merged entities

the omitted and replacement mentions having very similar informational content.

As expected, the scores in Category 3 are lower then those in Category 2 (as a whole), but they are still consistently better than the scores of the Category 2b.

4.1.4 Category 4: Unsuccessful coreference resolution

The entities in this category (Table 5) are divided into two subcategories:

No response entity has been given Two of the key entities (MZ38 and NW4) were not aligned with any response entities, and not surprisingly all metrics agree that the CR precision, recall and F-score equal zero.

The response entities do not contain a single "heavy" mention that is correct Although the response entities in the remaining entity pairs are non-empty, an intuitive CR evaluation says there is not much sense in aligning near-vacuous mentions if the entity is otherwise wrong or empty. Already in the two rather simple cases of WB0 and WB1 the metrics show large discrepancies: While link-based MUC and BLANC correctly give an F-score of 0.00 as there are no correct links in the entity, the mention-based B^3 and CEAF measures award them

Key entities	Response entities		MUC	B^3	$CEAF_e$	$CEAF_m$	BLANC
WB0							
• the beauty industry • it	• the one hand • it	P R F	0.00 0.00 0.00	50.00 50.00 50.00	50.00 50.00 50.00	50.00 50.00 50.00	0.00 0.00 0.00
WB1							
• the consumer • they	• clinical dermatologists • they	P R F	0.00 0.00 0.00	50.00 50.00 50.00	50.00 50.00 50.00	50.00 50.00 50.00	0.00 0.00 0.00
MZ33							
• Chang, Mei-liang, chairperson of the TBAD Women's Division, • her • she • Her • she	• her • she • Her	P R F	100.00 50.00 66.67	100.00 60.00 75.00	75.00 75.00 75.00	100.00 60.00 75.00	100.00 30.00 46.15

Table 5: Category 4: Unsuccessful coreference resolution

Entity	MUC	B^3	$CEAF_e$	$CEAF_m$	BLANC	Human
BC45	6	5	5	5	5	7
BC22	8	7	7	7	8	8
BC51	1	1	1	1	1	1
BN0	1	1	1	1	1	1
BN1	5	8	8	8	7	13
BN2	**13**	18	18	18	**13**	15
MZ19	10	10	10	10	10	14
MZ33	8	9	9	9	9	17
MZ17	**13**	17	17	17	**13**	15
MZ40	12	12	12	12	12	17
MZ22	**13**	13	13	13	**13**	10
MZ24	1	1	1	1	1	1
MZ38	–	**19**	**19**	**19**	**13**	**19**
NW0	**13**	**19**	**19**	**19**	**13**	10
NW1	10	10	10	10	10	8
NW2	7	6	6	6	6	5
NW3	1	1	1	1	1	1
NW4	–	**19**	**19**	**19**	**13**	**19**
NW5	**13**	13	13	13	**13**	10
WB0	**13**	13	13	13	**13**	**19**
WB1	**13**	13	13	13	**13**	**19**

Table 6: Ranking of our example entities.

with a rather high F-score of 50.00.

Entity MZ33 has been awarded high F-scores by all metrics, averaging 67.56%. However, almost all information from the key entity in MZ33 has been lost in the response entity: The key entity contains information on a person, a female, a Taiwanese national, her name (`Chang Mei-lian`) and the additional information that she is a `chairperson of the TBAD, Women's Division`. The response entity contains the information that its mentions refer to a female, which is most probably a person, but might be a ship, or a well loved pet. None of the metrics indicate that such a substantial loss of information renders the coreference resolution of MZ33 practically useless for a human user.

5 Entity ranking

As some of the metrics yield consistently lower F-score levels, it is more appropriate to compare rankings of entities than the actual F-scores (Table 6). We have also – to infuse an iota of old-school armchair linguistics – added a sixth rating column, showing intuitive rankings, based on informational value retained. The lowest rankings for any metric are marked in **bold**.

The entities showing broad agreement among the metrics are only the best (Category 1) and the worst ones (MZ38 and NW4, Category 4).

The metrics disagreement surfaces with entities WB0 and WB1 of Category 4. The link-based metrics, MUC and BLANC, rank them last (13th), while they are ranked much higher (13th out of 19) by the mention-based and entity-based metrics (B^3 and CEAF). In this case the human evaluator agrees with the link-based metrics: If there is not a single correct link within an entity, our intuition says that no useful CR has taken place.

However, the presence of a single correct coreferent link is not sufficient for our intuition of successful resolution. Consider entities MZ22 and NW5 (Table 3): They also consist of two entities where only one is correct, and have received the same ratings as WB0 and WB1, but in this case we judge CR as much more successful. There are two main differences between this and the previous case. Firstly, the correct mention is in the previous case a meaning-lean pronoun (`it` and `they`) while the correct mention in this case is a 'full-bodied' NP (`the school in Shenzhen` and `the delegation from China's People's Congress`). In addition, in both of the Category 2 entity pairs, the incorrect mention holds an informational value very close or identical to that of the correct mention. This example illustrates the importance of informational value content of the mentions for the human evaluation of the resolution.

6 Formalizing the intuition

We have earlier (§4.1) introduced a classificaion based on an informal notion of (human) intuitive coreference resolution evaluation. In this section we will try to formalize the classification.

Category 1 The key entities and response entities are identical:

$$\forall x(x \in K \leftrightarrow x \in R) \quad (1)$$

Category 2 The response entity is a proper subset of the key entity:

$$\begin{aligned} &\forall x(x \in R \rightarrow x \in K) \wedge \\ &\exists y(y \in K \wedge y \notin R) \end{aligned} \quad (2a)$$

This is the only condition for Category 2a. Category 2b shares the condition (2a), but to formalize it, we have to add *overlap(x,y)* relation. We can define it as a common substring for x and y of a certain length, possibly including at least one major syntactic category, or even the lexical 'head' if some way of operationalizing that notion is available.

$$\begin{aligned} &\exists x(x \in K \wedge x \in R) \wedge \\ &\exists y \exists z(y \in K \wedge z \in R \wedge overlap(y, z)) \end{aligned} \quad (2b)$$

We need at least two correct mentions in the response entity, and at least one that overlaps, as response entities containing only one correct mention do not have any correct links.

Category 3 Response entity contains a subset of the key entity mentions as well as additional mention(s) belonging to some other entity (E):

$$\begin{aligned} &\exists x(x \in K \wedge x \in R) \wedge \\ &\exists y(y \notin K \wedge y \in R \wedge y \in E) \end{aligned} \quad (3)$$

Category 4 The entities belonging to this category have a twofold definition: The response entity is either empty or if it contains one correct mention, it cannot contain an overlapping mention.

$$\begin{aligned} &\forall x(x \in K \rightarrow x \notin R) \vee \\ &\exists x(x \in K \wedge x \in R) \rightarrow \\ &\forall y \forall z((y \in K \wedge z \in R) \rightarrow \neg overlap(y, z)) \end{aligned} \quad (4)$$

The classification that has been introduced as a informal one in §4.1 is thus computable given an operational definition of overlap. In future work we will investigate the distribution of the four error categories on a larger sample.

7 Conclusion and outlook

In this paper we have compared metrics on the basis of their evaluation of coreference resolution performed on real-life texts, and contrasted their evaluation to an intuitive human evaluation of coreference resolution. We conjecture that humans require both correct coreferent links and correct (whole or partial) mentions of a certain information weight to consider a resolution successful.

This approach has some shortcomings. Firstly, the manual nature of the analysis has imposed a limit on the number of the examples, so our data may not be representative. Secondly, there is uncertainity connected to how well the coreference resolution evaluation metrics are suited to be used in this way. The latter drawback is the more serious one: the metrics were not designed to evaluate single key/response pairs, but whole texts. However, we would argue that if we want to discover new insights into the evaluation process, some level of approximation is necessary. There are at least two arguments in favor of this particular approximation: Firstly, all metrics are based on evaluating key/response pairs. Analyzing their performance at this level can be a reasonable indicator of their performance on the text level. Secondly, even if metrics are treated "unfairly", they are all treated equally.

We thus believe that this work can be seen as an illustration of remaining evaluation challenges in the field of coreference resolution.

A natural extension of this work would be including more humans in evaluating coreference resolution systems, to provide a more representative human judgement. This evaluation should then be extended from evaluating coreference resolution of single key/response entity pairs, to assessing the quality of coreference resolution on a text as a whole.

And, finally: Every mention carries an information value, and this weight varies from quite heavy (as in `vice-chief committee member Jiyun Tian`), to somewhat lighter (`Jiyun Tian`) to virtually weightless (`He`). Information weights are not distributed randomly, but conform to discourse structure. It would be interesting to map the pattern of their distribution, and see if incorporating this information could improve both coreference resolution and its quantitative evaluation.

8 Acknowledgements

We would like to thank the anonymous reviewers for their useful comments.

References

Amit Bagga and Breck Baldwin. 1998. Algorithms for scoring coreference chains. In *The First International Conference on Language Resources and Evaluation Workshop on Linguistics Coreference*, pages 563 – 566, Granada, Spain.

Pascal Denis and Jason Baldridge. 2009. Global joint models for coreference resolution and named entity classication. *Procesamiento del Lenguaje Natural*, 42:87–96.

Heeyoung Lee, Yves Peirsman, Angel Chang, Nathanael Chambers, Mihai Surdeanu, and Dan Jurafsky. 2011. Stanford's multi-pass sieve coreference resolution system at the CoNLL-2011 Shared Task. In *Proceedings of the 15th Conference on Computational Natural Language Learning: Shared Task*, pages 28–34, Portland, Oregon.

Xiaoqiang Luo, Abe Ittycheriah Hongyan Jing, Nanda Kambhatla, and Salim Roukos. 2004. A mention-synchronous coreference resolution algorithm based on the Bell tree. In *Proceedings of the 42nd Annual Meeting of the Association for Computational Linguistics*, pages 136–143, Barcelona, Spain.

Xiaoqiang Luo. 2005. On coreference resolution performance metrics. In *Proceedings of Human Language Technology Conference and Conference on Empirical Methods in Natural Language Processing (HLT/EMNLP)*, pages 25–32, Vancouver, Canada.

Sameer Pradhan, Lance Ramshaw, Mitchell Marcus, Martha Palmer, Ralph Weischedel, and Nianwen Xue. 2011. CoNLL-2011 Shared Task: Modeling unrestricted coreference in OntoNotes. In *Proceedings of the 15th Conference on Computational Natural Language Learning: Shared Task*, pages 1–27, Portland, Oregon.

Sameer Pradhan, Alessandro Moschitti, Nianwen Xue, Olga Uryupina, and Yuchen Zhang. 2012. CoNLL-2012 Shared Task: Modeling multilingual unrestricted coreference in OntoNotes. In *Proceedings of the Joint Conference on EMNLP and CoNLL: Shared Task*, pages 1–40, Jeju Island, Korea.

W. M. Rand. 1971. Objective criteria for evaluation of clustering methods. *Journal of American Statistical Association*, 66(336):846–850.

Marta Recasens and Eduard Hovy. 2011. BLANC: Implementing the Rand index for coreference evaluation. *Natural Language Engineering*, 17(04):485–510.

Marta Recasens, Lluis Màrquez, Emili Sapena, M. Antònia Marti, Mariona Taulé, Véronique Hoste, Massimo Poesio, and Yannick Versley. 2010. Semeval-2010 task 1: Coreference resolution in multiple languages. In *Proceedings of the 5th International Workshop on Semantic Evaluation, ACL 2010*, pages 1–8, Uppsala, Sweden.

Marc Vilain, John Burger, John Aberdeen, Dennis Connolly, and Lynette Hirschman. 1995. A model-theoretic coreference scoring scheme. In *Proceedings of the Sixth Message understanding Conference (MUC-6)*, pages 45–52, San Francisco, CA.

Xiaofeng Yang, Guodong Zhou, Jian Su, and Chew Lim Tan. 2003. Coreference resolution using competition learning approach. In *Proceedings of the 41st Annual Meeting of the Association for Computational Linguistics*, pages 176–183, Sapporo, Japan.

Reducing Annotation Effort on Unbalanced Corpus based on Cost Matrix

Wencan Luo, Diane Litman
Department of Computer Science
University of Pittsburgh
Pittsburgh, PA 15260, USA
{wencan,litman}@cs.pitt.edu

Joel Chan
Department of Psychology
University of Pittsburgh
Pittsburgh, PA 15260, USA
chozen86@gmail.com

Abstract

Annotated corpora play a significant role in many NLP applications. However, annotation by humans is time-consuming and costly. In this paper, a high recall predictor based on a cost-sensitive learner is proposed as a method to semi-automate the annotation of unbalanced classes. We demonstrate the effectiveness of our approach in the context of one form of unbalanced task: annotation of transcribed human-human dialogues for presence/absence of uncertainty. In two data sets, our cost-matrix based method of uncertainty annotation achieved high levels of recall while maintaining acceptable levels of accuracy. The method is able to reduce human annotation effort by about 80% without a significant loss in data quality, as demonstrated by an extrinsic evaluation showing that results originally achieved using manually-obtained uncertainty annotations can be replicated using semi-automatically obtained uncertainty annotations.

1 Introduction

Annotated corpora are crucial for the development of statistical-based NLP tools. However, the annotation of corpora is most commonly done by humans, which is time-consuming and costly. To obtain a higher quality annotated corpus, it is necessary to spend more time and money on data annotation. For this reason, one often has to accept some tradeoff between data quality and human effort.

A significant proportion of corpora are unbalanced, where the distribution of class categories are heavily skewed towards one or a few categories. Unbalanced corpora are common in a number of different tasks, such as emotion detection (Ang et al., 2002; Alm et al., 2005), sentiment classification (Li et al., 2012), polarity of opinion (Carvalho et al., 2011), uncertainty and correctness of student answers in tutoring dialogue systems (Forbes-Riley and Litman, 2011; Dzikovska et al., 2012), text classification (Forman, 2003), information extraction (Hoffmann et al., 2011), and so on[1].

In this paper, we present a semi-automated annotation method that can reduce annotation effort for the class of binary unbalanced corpora. Here is our proposed annotation scheme: the first step is to build a high-recall classifier with some initial annotated data with an acceptable accuracy via a cost-sensitive approach. The second step is to apply this classifier to the rest of the unlabeled data, where the data are then classified with positive or negative labels. The last step is to manually check every positive label and correct it if it is wrong.

To apply this method to work in practice, two research questions have to be addressed. The first one is how to get a high-recall classifier. High recall means only a low proportion of true positives are misclassified (false negatives). This property allows for only positive labels to be corrected by human annotators in the third step, so that annotation effort may be reduced. A related and separate research question concerns the overall quality of data when false negatives are not corrected: will a dataset annotated with this method produce the same results as a

[1] The unbalanced degrees - proportion of minority class category, of these corpora range from 3% to 24%.

Proceedings of the NAACL HLT 2013 Student Research Workshop, pages 8–15,
Atlanta, Georgia, 13 June 2013.

fully manually annotated version of the same dataset when analyzed for substantive research questions?

In this paper, we will answer the two research questions in the context of one form of binary unbalanced task[2]: annotation of transcribed human-human dialogue for presence/absence of uncertainty.

The contribution of this paper is twofold. First, an extrinsic evaluation demonstrates the utility of our approach, by showing that results originally achieved using manually-obtained uncertainty annotations can be replicated using semi-automatically obtained uncertainty annotations. Second, a high recall predictor based on a cost-sensitive learner is proposed as a method to semi-automate the annotation of unbalanced classes such as uncertainty.

2 Related Work

2.1 Reducing Annotation Effort

A number of semi-supervised learning methods have been proposed in the literature for reducing annotation effort, such as active learning (Cohn et al., 1994; Zhu and Hovy, 2007; Zhu et al., 2010), co-training (Blum and Mitchell, 1998) and self-training (Mihalcea, 2004). Active learning reduces annotation by carefully selecting more useful samples. Co-training relies on several conditional independent classifiers to tag new unlabeled data and self-training takes the advantage of full unlabeled data. These semi-supervised learning methods demonstrate that with a small proportion of annotated data, a classifier can achieve comparable performance with all annotated data. However, these approaches still need considerable annotation effort when a large corpus has to be annotated. In that case, all predicted labels have to be rechecked by humans manually. In addition, none of them take advantage of unbalanced data.

Another class of effort reduction techniques is pre-annotation, which uses supervised machine-learning systems to automatically assign labels to the whole data and subsequently lets human annotators correct them (Brants and Plaehn, 2000; Chiou et al., 2001; Xue et al., 2002; Ganchev et al., 2007; Chou et al., 2006; Rehbein et al., 2012).

Generally speaking, our annotation method belongs to the class of pre-annotation methods. However, our method improves pre-annotation for unbalanced data in two ways. Firstly, we lower the threshold for achieving a high recall classifier. Secondly, with pre-annotation, although people only perform a binary decision of whether the automatic classifier is either right or wrong, they have to go through all the unlabeled data one by one. In contrast, in our scheme, people go through only the positive predictions, which are much less than the whole unlabeled data, due to the unbalanced structure of the data. What's more, reducing the annotation effort is the goal of this paper but not building a high recall classifier such as Prabhakaran et al. (2012) and Ambati et al. (2010).

The approach proposed by Tetreault and Chodorow (2008) is similar to us. However, they assumed they had a high recall classifier but did not explicitly show how to build it. In addition, they did not provide extrinsic evaluation to see whether a corpus generated by pre-annotation is good enough to be used in real applications.

2.2 Uncertainty Prediction

Uncertainty is a lack of knowledge about internal state (Pon-Barry and Shieber, 2011). In this paper, we only focus on detection of uncertainty on text. Commonly used features are lexical features such as unigram (Forbes-Riley and Litman, 2011). Moreover, energy, dialogue features such as turn number, tutor goal, and metadata like gender are also considered by Forbes-Riley and Litman (2011). Uncertainty prediction is both substantively interesting (Chan et al., 2012; Forbes-Riley and Litman, 2009) and pragmatically expeditious for our purposes, due to its binary classification and typical unbalanced class structure.

CoNLL 2010 has launched a shared task to detect hedges and their scope in natural language text on two data sets: BioScope and Wikipedia (CoNLL, 2010). This first task to detect whether there is a hedge present or not present in a sentence is very similar to our uncertainty prediction task. 23 teams participated in the shared task with the best recall of 0.8772 on the BioScope, and 0.5528 on the Wikipedia. As we can see, uncertainty detection is not trivial and it can be hard to get a high recall classifier.

In this paper, we focus on lexical features for our

[2]This annotation scheme can also benefit other kinds of tasks.

purpose because lexical features are simple to extract and sufficient for our scheme. Even though other features may improve uncertainty prediction performance, with the goal of reducing annotation effort, such lexical features are shown to be good enough for our task.

3 The Corpora

We examine the following two data sets: the Mars Exploration Rover (MER) mission (Tollinger et al., 2006; Paletz and Schunn, 2011) and the student engineering team (Eng) dataset (Jang and Schunn, 2012). The MER scientists are evaluating data downloaded from the Rover, discussing their work process, and/or making plans for the Rovers. They come from a large team of about 100+ scientists/faculty, graduate students, and technicians. At any one time, conversations are between 2-10 people. The Eng teams are natural teams of college undergraduates working on their semester-long product design projects. The conversations involve 2-6 individuals. Audio and video are available for both data sets and transcripts are obtained with human annotators.

Our task is to annotate the transcribed human-human dialogues for presence/absence of uncertainty in each utterance. There are 12,331 transcribed utterances in the MER data set, and 44,199 transcribed utterances in the Eng data set. Both data sets are unbalanced: in the MER data, 1641 of all the 12,331 (13.3%) utterances are annotated as uncertain by trained human annotators; in the Eng data, only 1558 utterances are annotated, 221 of which are annotated as uncertain (14.2%). 96.5% of the utterances in the Eng data set have not been annotated yet, raising the need for an efficient annotated technique. Both data sets are annotated by two trained coders with high inter-rater agreement, at Cohen's kappa of 0.75 (Cohen, 1960). A sample dialogue snippet from the MER corpus is shown in Table 1. The last column indicates whether the utterance is labeled as uncertainty or not: '1' means uncertainty and '0' means certainty.

The MER data serves as the initial annotated set and a high recall classifier will be trained on it; the Eng data[3] serves as a simulated unlabeled data set to test the performance of our annotation scheme.

speaker	utterance	uncertainty?
S6	You can't see the forest through the trees.	0
S1	Yea, we never could see the [missing words]	1
S6	No we had to get above it	0
S4	We just went right through it	0
S6	Yea	0
S1	I still don't,	0
	I'm not quite sure	1

Table 1: Sample dialogue from the MER corpus

4 High Recall Classifier

4.1 Basic Classifier

The uncertainty prediction problem can be viewed as a binary classification problem. It involves two steps to build a high recall classifier for unbalanced data. The first step is to build up a simple classifier; the second step is to augment this classifier to favor high recall.

Aiming for a simple classifier with high recall, only some lexical words/phrases are used as features here. There are several resources for the words/phrases of uncertainty prediction. The main resource is a guideline book used by our annotators showing how to distinguish uncertainty utterance. It gives three different kinds of words/phrases, shown in Table 2 indicated by three superscripts '+', '-' and '*'. The words/phrases with '+' show some evidence of uncertainty; ones with '-' mean that they show no evidence of uncertainty; others with '*' may or may not show uncertainty. The second source is from existing literature. The words/phrases with '1' are from (Hiraishi et al., 2000) and ones with '2' are from (Holms, 1999).

For each word/phrase w, a binary feature is used to indicate whether the word/phrase w is in the utterance or not.

A Naive Bayes classifier is trained on the MER data using these features and tested on the Eng data. The performances of the model on the train set and test set are shown in Table 3. Both weighted and unweighted false positive (FP) Rate, Precision, Recall and F-Measure are reported. However, in later experiments, we will focus on only the positive class (the uncertainty class). A 0.689 recall means that 510 out of 1641 positive utterances are missed using this model.

[3]The Eng data in this paper denotes the annotated subset of the original Eng corpus.

as far as^{+}	i hope^{+}	somehow^{+}	it will^{-}	don't remember*	maybe*	tends to*	doubtful^{1}
as far as i know^{+}	i think^{+}	something^{+}	it wont^{-}	essentially*	most*	that can vary*	good chance^{1}
as far as we know^{+}	i thought^{+}	something like this^{+}	it would^{-}	fairly*	mostly*	typically*	improbable^{1}
believe^{+}	i wont^{+}	worried that^{+}	would it be^{-}	for the most part*	normally*	uh*	possible^{1}
could^{+}	im not sure^{+}	you cannot tell^{+}	about*	frequently*	pretty much*	um*	probable^{1}
guess^{+}	may^{+}	can^{-}	almost*	generally*	quite*	usually*	relatively^{1}
guessed^{+}	might^{+}	i am^{-}	any nonprecise amount*	hes*	should*	very*	roughly^{1}
guessing^{+}	not really^{+}	i can^{-}	basically*	hopefully*	sometimes*	virtually*	tossup^{1}
i believe^{+}	not sure^{+}	i will^{-}	believed*	i assumed that*	somewhat*	whatever*	unlikely^{1}
i cant really^{+}	possibly^{+}	i would^{-}	cannot remember*	it sounds as*	somewhere*	you know*	of course^{2}
i feel^{+}	probably^{+}	it can^{-}	can't remember*	kind of*	stuff*	almost certain^{1}	sort of^{2}
i guess^{+}	really^{+}	it is^{-}	do not remember*	likely*	tend to*	almost impossible^{1}	

Table 2: Words/phrases for uncertainty prediction.

Data Set	FP Rate	Precision	Recall	F-Measure	Class
MER	.311	.954	.989	.971	0
	.011	.908	.689	.784	1
	.271	.948	.949	.946	(Weighted)
Eng	.475	.926	.981	.952	0
	.019	.817	.525	.639	1
	.41	.91	.916	.803	(Weighted)

Table 3: Naive Bayes classifier performance on the MER (train set) and Eng (test set) with only the words/phrases

assume	I didn't know	more or less	some kind
couldn't	i don't even know	no idea	suppose
don't know	if	not clear	suspect
don't think	if it	or	think
don't understand	if we	perhaps	thought
doubt	if you	possibility	unclear
either	imagine	potential	what i understood
figured	kinda	presumably	wondering
i bet	kinds of	seem	
i can try	like	some	

Table 4: New words/phrases for uncertainty prediction

After error analysis, a few new words/phrases are added to the feature set, shown in Table 4. By supplementing the original feature set in this way, we reran the training yielding our final baseline, the performance on the training data (MER) and testing data (Eng) is shown in Table 5. This time, we compare different classifiers including Naive Bayes (NB), Decision Tree (DT) and Support Vector Machine (SVM). All of them are implemented using the open source platform Weka (Hall et al., 2009) with default parameters.

As we can see, test recall is worse than train recall.

Data Set	Method	TP	FP	Precision	Recall	F-Measure
MER	NB	.732	.016	.875	.732	.797
	DT	.831	.013	.908	.831	.868
	SVM	.811	.013	.905	.811	.855
Eng	NB	.679	.014	.888	.679	.769
	DT	.665	.021	.84	.665	.742
	SVM	.674	.022	.832	.674	.745

Table 5: Performance with original and new words/phrases as a feature set: train on the MER and test on the Eng data for class '1'. TP is true positive; FP is false positive

In addition, although DT and SVM perform better than NB on train data set, they have similar performance on the test set. Thus, the performance of the baseline is not unacceptable, but neither is it stellar. In advance, it is not hard to build such a model, since only simple features and classifiers are used here.

4.2 Augmenting the Classifier using a Cost Matrix

In our annotation framework, if the classifier achieves 100% recall, the annotated data will be perfect because all the wrong predictions can be corrected. That's the reason why we are seeking for a high recall classifier. A confusion matrix, is a common way to represent classifier performance. High recall is indexed by a low false negative (FN) rate; therefore, we aim to minimize FNs to achieve high recall.

Following this idea, we employ a cost-sensitive model, where the cost of FN is more than false positive (FP).

Following the same notation, we represent our cost-sensitive classifier as a cost matrix. In our cost matrix, classifying an actual class '1' as '1' costs C_{tp}, an actual class '0' as '1' costs C_{fp}, an actual class '1' to '0' costs C_{fn}, and '0' to '0' costs C_{tn}. To achieve a high recall, C_{fn} should be more than C_{fp}.

We can easily achieve 100% recall by classifying all samples to '1', but this would defeat our goal of reducing human annotation effort, since all utterance uncertainty predictions would need to be manually corrected. Thus, at the same time of a high recall, we should also balance the total ratio of TP and FP.

In our experiment, C_{tp} and C_{tn} are set to 0 since they are perfectly correct. Additionally, $C_{fp} = 1$ all the time and C_{fn} changes with different scales. FPs

C_{fn}	FP Rate	Precision	Recall	F-Measure	$(TP + FP)/N$
1	.022	.831	.67	.742	.114
2	.024	.825	.683	.748	.117
3	.037	.771	.747	.759	.138
5	.052	.726	.828	.774	.162
10	.071	.674	.887	.766	.187
15	.091	.622	.91	.739	.207
20	.091	.622	.91	.739	.207

Table 6: Test performance with cost matrix

mean wrong predictions, but we can correct them during the second pass to check them. However, we cannot correct FNs without going through the whole data set, so they are a more egregious detriment to the quality of the annotated data. During the experiment, C_{fn} varies from 1 to 20. With increases in C_{fn}, the cost of FN increases compared to FP.

The cost-sensitive classifier is relying on Weka with reweighting training instances. In this task, SVM performed better than NB and DT. Only SVM results are included here due to space constraint. The test results are shown in Table 6[4]. The last column in the two tables is the total proportion of positive predictions $(FP + TP)$. This value indicates the total amount of data that humans have to check in the second pass to verify whether positive predictions are correct. To reduce human annotation effort, we would like this value to be as low as possible.

As shown in Table 6, with the increase of C_{fn}, the recall increases; however, the proportion of positive predictions also increases. Therefore, it is a tradeoff to achieve a high recall and a low ratio of TP and FP.

For the test set, the recall increases with larger C_{fn}, even with a small increase of C_{fn} from 1 to 3. Remarkably, the classifier gives us a high recall while keeping the proportion of positive predictions at an acceptably low level. When $C_{fn} = 20$ for the test set, only 20.7% of the data need to be manually checked by humans, and less than 10% uncertain utterances (19 out of 221 for the Eng data) are missed.

Now, we have achieved a high recall classifier with an acceptable ratio of positive predictions.

5 Extrinsic Evaluation of Semi-Automated Annotation

Even with a high recall classifier, some of the true positive data are labeled incorrectly in the final annotated corpus. In addition, it also changes the distribution of class labels.

To test whether it hurts the overall data quality, we performed an analysis, which demonstrates that this annotation scheme is sufficient to produce quality data. We attempted to replicate an analysis on the Eng data set, which examines the use of analogy, a cognitive strategy where a source and target knowledge structure are compared in terms of structural correspondences as a strategy for solving problems under uncertainty. The analysis we attempt to replicate here focuses on examining how uncertainty levels change relative to baseline before, during, and after the use of analogies.

The overall Eng transcripts were segmented into one of 5 block types: 1) pre-analogy (Lag -1) blocks, 10 utterances just prior to an analogy episode, 2) during-analogy (Lag 0) blocks, utterances from the beginning to end of an analogy episode, 3) post-analogy (Lag 1) blocks, 10 utterances immediately following an analogy episode, 4) post-post-analogy (Lag 2) blocks, 10 utterances immediately following post-analogy utterances, and 5) baseline blocks, each block of 10 utterances at least 25 utterances away from the other block types. The measure of uncertainty in each block was the proportion of uncertain utterances. The sampling strategy for the baseline blocks was designed to provide an estimate of uncertainty levels when the speakers were engaged in pre-analogy, during-analogy, or post-analogy conversation, with the logic being that a certain amount of lag or spillover of uncertainty was assumed to take place surrounding analogy episodes.

Figure 1 shows the relationship of block type to mean levels of uncertainty, comparing the pattern with human vs. classifier-supported uncertainty labels. The classifier-generated labels were first preprocessed such that all FPs were removed, but FNs remain. This re-analysis comparison thus provides a test of whether the recall rate is high enough that known statistical effects are not substantially altered or removed. To examine how different settings of C_{fn} might impact overall performance, we used labels (corrected for false positives) for 4 different levels of C_{fn} (1, 5, 10, 20) from the Table 6.

In the Eng data analyses, the main findings were that analogy was triggered by local spikes in uncertainty levels (Lag -1 > baseline), replicating re-

[4]Only $C_{fn} = 1, 2, 3, 5, 10, 15, 20$ are reported here due to page limits

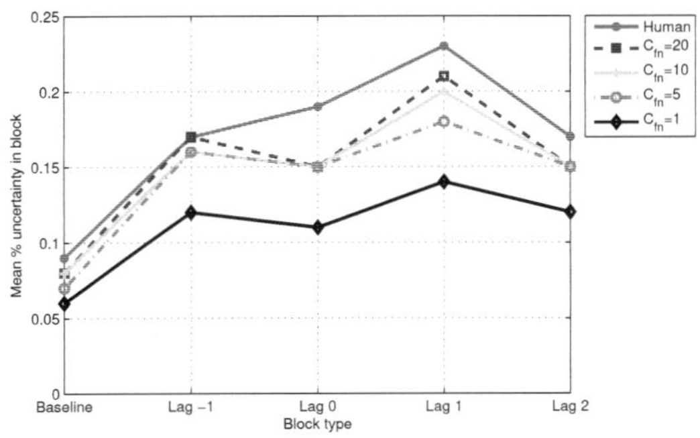

Figure 1: Mean % uncertainty by block type and label source (Eng data set)

Table 7: Standardized mean difference (Cohen's d) from baseline by block type and label source (the Eng data set) (Note: '*' denotes $p < .05$, '**' denotes $p < .01$)

	Block type			
	Lag -1	Lag 0	Lag 1	Lag 2
Human	0.54*	0.4	0.79**	0.46*
$C_{fn} = 20$	0.57*	0.3	0.78**	0.44
$C_{fn} = 10$	0.58**	0.32	0.73**	0.47*
$C_{fn} = 5$	0.57*	0.34	0.66**	0.48*
$C_{fn} = 1$	0.42	0.25	0.54*	0.40

sults from prior work with the MER dataset (Chan et al., 2012); in contrast to the findings in MER, uncertainty did not reduce to baseline levels following analogy (Lags 1 and 2 > baseline). Figure 1 plots the relationship of block type to mean levels of uncertainty in this data set, comparing the pattern with human vs. classifier-generated uncertainty labels. Table 7 shows the standardized mean difference (Cohen's d) (Cohen, 1988) from baseline by block type and label source. The pattern of effects (Lag -1 > baseline, Lags 1 and 2 > baseline) remains substantially unchanged with the exception of the Lag 2 vs. baseline comparison falling short of statistical significance (although note that the standardized mean difference remains very similar) for C_{fn} ranging from 20 to 5, although we can observe a noticeable attenuation of effect sizes from C_{fn} of 5 and below, and a loss of statistical significance for the main effect of uncertainty being significantly higher than baseline for Lag -1 blocks when $C_{fn} = 1$.

The re-analysis clearly demonstrates that the recall rate of the classifier is sufficient to not substantially alter or miss known statistical effects. We can reasonably extrapolate that using this classifier for uncertainty annotation in other datasets should be satisfactory.

6 Conclusion and Discussion

In this paper, a simple high recall classifier is proposed based on a cost matrix to semi-automate the annotation of corpora with unbalanced classes. This classifier maintains a good balance between high recall and high FP and NP ratio. In this way, humans can employ this classifier to annotate new data with significantly reduced effort (approximately 80% less effort, depending on the degree of imbalance in the data). Although the classifier does introduce some misclassified samples to the final annotation, an extrinsic evaluation demonstrates that the recall rate is high enough and the performance does not sacrifice data quality.

Like other semi-supervised or supervised methods for supporting annotation, our annotation scheme has some limitations that should be noted. Firstly, an initial annotated data set is needed to derive a good performance classifier and the amount of annotated data is dependent on the specific task[5]. Secondly, the features and machine learning algorithms used in semi-supervised annotation are also domain specific. At the same time, there are some unique challenges and opportunities that can be further investigated for our annotation scheme on unbalanced data. For example, even though the cost matrix method can achieve a high recall for binary classification problem, whether it can be generalized to other tasks (e.g., multi-class classification tasks) is an unanswered question. Another open question is how the degree of unbalance between classes in the corpora affects overall annotation quality. We suggest that if the data is not unbalanced, the total amount of effort that can be reduced will be lower.

Acknowledgments

The collection of the engineering data was supported by NSF grants SBE-0738071, SBE-0823628, and SBE-0830210. Analogy analysis was supported by NSF grant SBE-1064083.

[5]For a new task, a new feature set is usually derived.

References

Cecilia Ovesdotter Alm, Dan Roth and Richard Sproat. 2005. *Emotions from text: Machine learning for text-based emotion prediction.* In Proceedings of HLT/EMNLP 2005.

Bharat Ram Ambati, Mridul Gupta, Samar Husain and Dipti Misra Sharma. 2010. *A high recall error identification tool for Hindi treebank validation.* In Proceedings of The 7th International Conference on Language Resources and Evaluation (LREC), Valleta, Malta.

Jeremy Ang, Rajdip Dhillon, Ashley Krupski, Elizabeth Shriberg and Andreas Stolcke. 2002. *Prosody-based automatic detection of annoyance and frustration in human-computer Dialog.* In INTERSPEECH-02.

Avrim Blum and Tom Mitchell. 1998. *Combining labeled and unlabeled data with co-training.* In Proceedings of the eleventh annual conference on Computational learning theory, p.92-100, July 24-26, Madison, Wisconsin, United States

Thorsten Brants and Oliver Plaehn. 2000. *Interactive corpus annotation.* In Proceedings of LREC-2000.

Paula Carvalho, Luís Sarmento, Jorge Teixeira and Mário J. Silva. 2011. *Liars and saviors in a sentiment annotated corpus of comments to political debates.* In Proceedings of the Association for Computational Linguistics (ACL 2011), Portland, OR.

Joel Chan, Susannah B. F. Paletz and Christian D. Schunn. 2012. *Analogy as a strategy for supporting complex problem solving under uncertainty.* Memory & Cognition, 40, 1352-1365.

Fu-Dong Chiou, David Chiang and Martha Palmer. 2001. *Facilitating treebank annotation using a statistical parser.* In HLT'01. ACL.

Wen-Chi Chou, Richard Tzong-Han Tsai, Ying-Shan Su, Wei Ku1, Ting-Yi Sung and Wen-Lian Hsu. 2006. *A semi-automatic method for annotating a biomedical proposition bank.* In Proceedings of FLAC-2006.

David Cohn, Richard Ladner and Alex Waibel. 1994. *Improving generalization with active learning.* Machine Learning, 15 (2), 201-221.

Jacob Cohen. 1960. *A coefficient of agreement for nominal scales.* Educational and Psychological Measurement, 20, 37-46.

Jacob Cohen. 1988. *Statistical power analysis for the behavioral sciences (2nd ed.).* Lawrence Erlbaum.

CoNLL-2010 Shared Task. 2010. In Fourteenth Conference on Computational Natural Language Learning, Proceedings of the Shared Task.

Myroslava Dzikovska, Peter Bell, Amy Isard and Johanna D. Moore. 2012. *Evaluating language understanding accuracy with respect to objective outcomes in a dialogue system.* EACL 2012: 471-481.

Kate Forbes-Riley and Diane Litman. 2009. *Adapting to student uncertainty improves tutoring dialogues.* In Proceedings 14th International Conference on Artificial Intelligence in Education (AIED2009), pp. 33-40.

Kate Forbes-Riley and Diane Litman. 2011. *Benefits and challenges of real-time uncertainty detection and adaptation in a spoken dialogue computer tutor.* Speech Communication, v53, pp. 1115-1136.

George Forman 2003. *An Extensive empirical study of feature selection metrics for text classification.* Journal of Machine Learning Research, 3, 1289-1305.

Kuzman Ganchev, Fernando Pereira, Mark Mandel, Steven Carroll and Peter White. 2007. *Semi-automated named entity annotation.* In Proceedings of the linguistic annotation workshop, pp. 53-56

Mark Hall, Eibe Frank, Geoffrey Holmes, Bernhard Pfahringer, Peter Reutemann and Ian H.Witten. 2009. *The WEKA data mining software: An update.* SIGKDD Explorations, 11(1).

Taka Hiraishi, Buruhani Nyenzi, Jim Penman and Semere Habetsion. 2000. *Quantifying uncertainties in practice.* In Revised 1996 IPCC guidelines for national greenhouse gas inventories.

Raphael Hoffmann, Congle Zhang, Xiao Ling, Luke Zettlemoyer and Daniel S. Weld. 2011. *Knowledge-based weak supervision for information extraction of overlapping relations.* In ACL.

Janet Holmes. 1999. *Women, men, and politeness.* London, SAGE publications, pp:86-96

Jooyoung Jang and Christian Schunn. 2012. *Physical design tools support and hinder innovative engineering design.* Journal of Mechanical Design, vol. 134, no. 4, pp. 041001-1-041001-9.

Shoushan Li, Shengfeng Ju, Guodong Zhou and Xiaojun Li. 2012. *Active learning for imbalanced sentiment classification.* EMNLP-CoNLL 2012: 139-148

Rada Mihalcea. 2004. *Co-training and self-training for word sense disambiguation.* In Proceedings of the 8th Conference on Computational Natural Language Learning (CoNLL, Boston, MA). 33-40.

Susannah B. F. Paletz and Christian D. Schunn. 2011. *Assessing group-level participation in fluid teams: Testing a new metric.* Behav Res 43:522-536.

Heather Pon-Barry and Stuart M. Shieber 2011. *Recognizing uncertainty in speech.* EURASIP Journal on Advances in Signal Processing.

Vinodkumar Prabhakaran, Michael Bloodgood, Mona Diab, Bonnie Dorr, Lori Levin, Christine D. Piatko, Owen Rambow and Benjamin Van Durme 2012 *Statistical modality tagging from rule-based annotations and crowdsourcing.* In Proceedings of ACL Workshop on Extra-propositional aspects of meaning in computational linguistics (ExProM).

Ines Rehbein, Josef Ruppenhofer and Caroline Sporleder. 2012. *Is it worth the effort? Assessing the benefits of partial automatic pre-labeling for frame-semantic annotation*. Language Resources and Evaluation, Vol.46, No.1. pp. 1-23

Joel R. Tetreault and Martin Chodorow. *Native judgments of non-native usage: experiments in preposition error detection*. In Proceedings of the Workshop on Human Judgements in Computational Linguistics, p.24-32, Manchester, United Kingdom.

Irene V. Tollinger, Christian D. Schunn and Alonso H. Vera. 2006. *What changes when a large team becomes more expert? Analyses of speedup in the Mars Exploration Rovers science planning process*. In Proceedings of the 28th Annual Conference of the Cognitive Science Society (pp. 840-845). Mahwah, NJ: Erlbaum.

Nianwen Xue, Fu-Dong Chiou and Martha Palmer. 2002. *Building a large-scale annotated chinese corpus*. In Proceedings of the 19th international conference on Computational linguistics. ACL.

Jingbo Zhu and Eduard Hovy. 2007. *Active learning for word sense disambiguation with methods for addressing the class imbalance problem*. In Proceedings of the 2007 Joint Conference on Empirical Methods in Natural Language Processing and Computational Natural Language Learning, 783-790.

Jingbo Zhu, Huizhen Wang, Eduard H. Hovy and Matthew Y. Ma. 2010. *Confidence-based stopping criteria for active learning for data annotation*. ACM Transactions on Speech and Language Processing, 6, 124.

A Machine Learning Approach to Automatic Term Extraction using a Rich Feature Set*

Merley da Silva Conrado, Thiago A. Salgueiro Pardo, and Solange Oliveira Rezende
Laboratory of Computational Intelligence,
An Interinstitutional Center for Research and Development in Computational Linguistic,
Institute of Mathematical and Computer Sciences,
University of Sao Paulo (USP),
P.O. Box 668, 13561-970, Sao Carlos-SP, Brazil
{merleyc,taspardo,solange}@icmc.usp.br

Abstract

In this paper we propose an automatic term extraction approach that uses machine learning incorporating varied and rich features of candidate terms. In our preliminary experiments, we also tested different attribute selection methods to verify which features are more relevant for automatic term extraction. We achieved state of the art results for unigram extraction in Brazilian Portuguese.

1 Introduction

Terms are terminological units from specialised texts (Castellví et al., 2001). A term may be: (i) simple[1] (a single element), such as "*biodiversity*", or (ii) complex (more than one element), such as "*aquatic ecosystem*" and "*natural resource management*".

Automatic term extraction (ATE) methods aim to identify terminological units in specific domain corpora (Castellví et al., 2001). Such information is extremely useful for several tasks, from the linguistic perspective of building dictionaries, taxonomies and ontologies, to computational applications as information retrieval, extraction, and summarisation.

Although ATE has been researched for more than 20 years, there is still room for improvement. There are four major ATE problems. The first one is that the ATE approaches may extract terms that are not actual terms ("noise") or do not extract actual terms ("silence"). Considering the ecology domain, an example of silence is when a term (e.g., *pollination*), with low frequency, is not considered a candidate term (CT), and, therefore, it will not appear in the extracted term list if we consider its frequency. Regarding noise, if we consider that nouns may be terms and that adjectives may not, if an adjective (e.g., *ecological*) is mistakenly tagged as a noun, it will be wrongly extracted as a term. The second problem is the difficulty in dealing with extremely high number of candidates (called the high dimensionality of candidate representation) that requires time to process them. Since the ATE approaches generate large lists of TCs, we have the third problem that is the time and human effort spent for validating the TCs, which usually is manually performed. The fourth problem is that the results are still not satisfactory and there is a natural ATE challenge since the difficulty in obtaining a consensus among the experts about which words are terms of a specific domain (Vivaldi and Rodríguez, 2007).

Our proposed ATE approach uses machine learning (ML), since it has been achieving high precision values (Zhang et al., 2008; Foo and Merkel, 2010; Zhang et al., 2010; Loukachevitch, 2012). Although ML may also generate noise and silence, it facilitates the use of a large number of TCs and their features, since ML techniques learn by themselves how to recognize a term and then they save time extracting them.

Our approach differs from others because we adopt a rich feature set using varied knowledge levels. With this, it is possible to decrease the silence and noise and, consequently, to improve the ATE results. Our features range from simple statistical (e.g., term frequency) and linguistic (e.g., part of

*This research was supported by FAPESP (Proc. No. 2009/16142-3 and 2012/09375-4), Brazil.

[1] When we refer to *unigrams*, we mean *simple terms*.

Proceedings of the NAACL HLT 2013 Student Research Workshop, pages 16–23,
Atlanta, Georgia, 13 June 2013.

speech - POS) knowledge to more sophisticated hybrid knowledge, such as the analysis of the term context. As far as we know, the combined use of this specific knowledge has not been applied before. Another difference is that we apply 3 statistical features (Term Variance (Liu et al., 2005), Term Variance Quality (Dhillon et al., 2003), and Term Contribution (Liu et al., 2003)) that to date have only been used for attribute selection and not for term extraction. As far as we know, the combined use of this specific knowledge and feature feedback has not been applied before. We also propose 4 new linguistic features for ATE. All these features are detailed in Section 4. Finally, for the first time, ML is being applied in the task of ATE in Brazilian Portuguese (BP) corpora. Our approach may also be easily adapted to other languages.

We focus on extracting only unigram terms, since this is already a complex task. We run our experiments on 3 different corpora. Our main contribution is the improvement of precision (in the best case, we improve the results 11 times) and F-measure (in the best case, we improve 2 times).

Section 2 presents the main related work. Section 3 describes our ATE approach. Section 4 details the experiments, and Section 5 reports the results. Conclusions and future work are presented in Section 6.

2 Related Work

There are several recent and interesting studies that are not focused on extracting unigrams (Estopà et al., 2000; Almeida and Vale, 2008; Zhang et al., 2008; Zhang et al., 2010; Nazar, 2011; Vivaldi et al., 2012; Lopes, 2012). Normally, ATE studies use corpora of different domain and language and, in some cases, the authors use different evaluation measures. Regardless of variation (e.g., the size of the test corpora), we mention studies that have highlighted results for **unigrams**[2]. When possible, we show the best precision (P) of the related work and its recall (R).

(Ventura and Silva, 2008) extracted terms using statistical measures that consider the predecessors and successors of TCs. They achieved, for English, P=81.5% and R=55.4% and, for Spanish, P=78.2% and R=60.8%. For Spanish, the Greek forms of a candidate and their prefix may help to extract terms (e.g., the Greek formant *laring* that belongs to the term ***laring****oespasm* in the medical domain) (Vivaldi and Rodríguez, 2007), achieving about P=55.4% and R=58.1%. For Spanish, (Gelbukh et al., 2010) compared TCs of a domain with words of a general corpus using Likelihood ratio based distance. They achieved P=92.5%. For Brazilian Portuguese, the ExPorTer methods are the only previous work that uniquely extract unigrams (Zavaglia et al., 2007). Therefore, they are the state of the art for unigrams extraction for BP. The linguistic ExPorTer considers terms that belong to some POS patterns and uses indicative phrases (such as *is defined as*) that may identify where terms are. It achieved P=2.74% and R=89.18%. The hybrid ExPorTer used these linguistic features with frequency and Likelihood ratio. The latter one obtained P=12.76% and R=23.25%.

3 Term Extraction Approach based on Machine Learning

In order to model the ATE task as a machine learning solution, we consider each word in the input texts[3] of a specific domain (except the stopwords) as a learning instance (candidate term). For each instance, we identify a set of features over which the classification is performed. The classification predicts which words are terms (unigrams) of a specific domain. We test different attribute selection methods in order to verify which features are more relevant to classify a term.

We start by preprocessing the input texts, as shown in Figure 1. This step consists of POS tagging the corpora and normalizing[4] the words of the texts. The normalization minimizes the second ATE problem because it allows working with a lower CT representation dimensionality. When working with a lower dimensionality, the words that do not help identify terms are eliminated. Consequently, fewer candidates should to be validated or refuted as terms (it would minimize the third ATE problem). When working with fewer candidates it also may improve the result quality (it handles the fourth ATE prob-

[2]It is not specified if (Zhang et al., 2010) extracted simple or complex terms.

[3]When we refer to *texts*, we mean *documents*.

[4]Normalization consists of standardizing the words by reducing their variations.

lem), and, definitely, it spends less time and fewer resources to carry out the experiments. By improving the results, consequently, we minimize silence and noise, which handles the first ATE problem. Afterwards, we remove stopwords.

In order to identify a set of features over which the classification is performed, we studied and tested several measures. The feature identification is the most important step of our approach. We divide the features into two types: (i) the features that obtain statistical, linguistic, and hybrid knowledge from the input corpus, such as TFIDF and POS, and (ii) the features that obtain these knowledge from measures that use other corpora besides the input corpus. The corpora belong to another domain that is different of the input corpus domain (called contrastive corpora) or not belong to any specific domain (called general corpora). Our hypothesis is that, with the joining of features of different levels of knowledge, it is possible to improve the ATE.

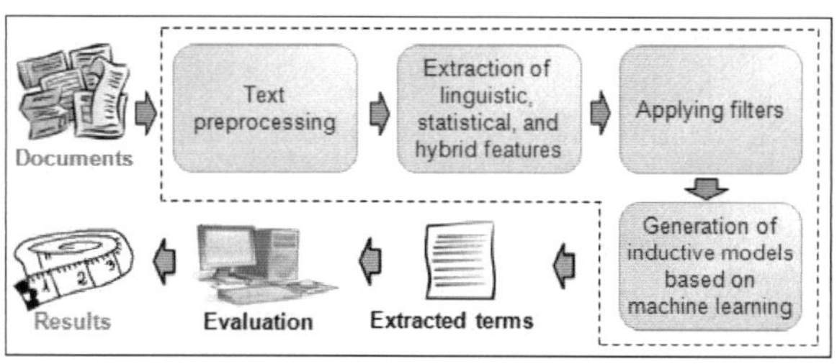

Figure 1: Term extraction approach proposed.

4 Experimental Setup

At this point, for obtaining the knowledge in order to extract terms, we tested 17 features that do not depend on general or contrastive corpora and 2 features that depend on these corpora. We intend to explore more features (and we will possibly propose new measures) that use contrastive or general corpora or any taxonomic structure. The experiments that expand the number of features are ongoing now.

We used 3 corpora of different domains in the Portuguese language. The EaD corpus (Souza and Di Felippo, 2010) has 347 texts about distance education and has a gold standard with 118 terms[5] (Gianoti and Di Felippo, 2011). The second one is the ECO[6] corpus (Zavaglia et al., 2007). It contains 390 texts of ecology domain and its gold standard has 322 unigrams. The latter is the Nanoscience and Nanotechnology (N&N) corpus (Coleti et al., 2008) that contains 1,057 texts. Its gold standard has 1,794 unigrams (Coleti et al., 2008; Coleti et al., 2009).

In order to preprocess these corpora, we POS tagged them using the PALAVRAS parser (Bick, 2000) and normalized their words using a stemming[7] technique. Stemming was chosen because of its capacity to group similar word meanings, and its use decreases representation dimensionality of candidate terms, which minimizes the second and third ATE problems. Afterwards, we removed the stopwords[8], the conjugation of the verb "to be", punctuation, numbers, accents, and the words composed of only one character are removed.

We identify and calculate 19 features in which 11 features are used for ATE in the literature, 3 features are normally applied to the attribute selection tasks (identified by *), 1 normally used for Named Entity Recognition (identified by **), and we created 4 new features (identified by $^{\Delta}$). These features are shown in Table 1, accompanied by the hypotheses that underlie their use. They are also divided into 3 levels of knowledge: statistical, linguistic, and hybrid.

For the ***S*** feature, we removed stopwords at the beginning and at the end of these phrases. For ***POS***, we assumed that terms may also be adjectives (Almeida and Vale, 2008), besides nouns and verbs. For ***GC*** and ***Freq_GC***, we used the NILC Corpus[9] as a general corpus, which contains 40 million words. We created and used 40 indicative phrases (***NPs***). For example, considering *are composed of* as an IP in *All organisms are composed of one or more cells*, we would consider *organisms* and *cells* as TCs. For features related to CT stem, we analyzed, e.g., the words *educative, educators, education* and *educate* that came from the stem *educ*. Therefore, *educ* may

[5](Gianoti and Di Felippo, 2011) stated that the EaD unigram gold standard has 59 terms, but in this paper we used 118 unigrams that the authors provided us prior to their work.

[6]ECO corpus - http://www.nilc.icmc.usp.br/nilc/projects/bloc-eco.htm

[7]PTStemmer: A Stemming toolkit for the Portuguese language - http://code.google.com/p/ptstemmer/

[8]Stoplist and Indicative Phrase list are avaiable in http://www2.icmc.usp.br/ merleyc/

[9]NILC Corpus - http://www.nilc.icmc.usp.br/nilc/tools/corpora.htm

Table 1: Features of candidate terms.

Feature	*Description*	*Hypothesis*
The eight linguistic features		
S	noun and prepositional phrases	terms are noun phrases and, sometimes, prepositional phrases
N_S	head of phrases	heads of noun and prepositional phrases
POS	noun, proper noun, and adjective	terms follow some patterns
IP	indicative phrases	IPs may identify definitions/descriptions that may be terms
N_noun $^{\Delta}$	number of nouns	stemmed terms come from higher number of nouns than adjectives or verbs
N_adj $^{\Delta}$	number of adjectives	
N_verb $^{\Delta}$	number of verbs	
N_PO $^{\Delta}$	total of words from which stemmed TCs come from	
The seven statistical features		
SG**	n-gram length	each domain has a term pattern
TF	Term Frequency	terms have neither low nor very high frequencies
DF	Document Frequency	terms appear in at least certain number of documents
TFIDF	Term Frequency Inverse Document Frequency (Salton and Buckley, 1987)	terms are very common in the corpus but they occur in few documents in this corpus
TCo*	Term Contribution (Liu et al., 2003)	terms help to distinguish the different documents
TV*	Term Variance (Liu et al., 2005)	terms do not have low frequency in documents and maintain a non-uniform distribution throughout corpus (higher variance)
TVQ*	Term Variance Quality (Dhillon et al., 2003)	
The four hybrid features		
GC	CT occurrence in general corpus	terms do not occur with high frequency in a general corpus
Freq_GC	CT frequency in GC	
C-value	the potential of a CT to be a term (Frantzi et al., 1998)	the C-value helps to extract terms
NC-value	CT context (Frantzi et al., 1998)	candidate context helps to extract terms

have as features ***N_Noun*** = 2 (*educators* and *education*), ***N_Adj*** = 1 *educative*, ***N_Verb*** = 1 (*educate*), and ***N_PO*** = 4 (total number of words). Our hypothesis is that stemmed candidates that were originated from a higher number of nouns than adjectives or verbs will be terms. Finally, we used NC-Value adapted to unigrams (Barrón-Cedeño et al., 2009).

After calculating the features for each unigram (candidate term), the CT representation has high dimensionality (it is the second ATE problem) and, hence, the experiments may take a considerable amount of time to be executed. To decrease this dimensionality and, consequently, the number of TCs (which corresponds to the second and third ATE problems, respectively), we tested two different cut-offs, which preserve only TCs that occur in at least two documents in the corpus. The first cut-off is called *C1*. In the second one (called *C2*), the candidates must be noun and prepositional phrases and also follow some of these POS: nouns, proper nouns, verbs, and adjectives. The number of obtained candidates (stems) was 10,524, 14,385, and 46,203, for the ECO, EaD, and N&N corpora, respectively. When using the *C1* cut-off, we decreased to 55,15%, 45,82%, and 57,04%, and *C2* decreased 63.10%, 63.18%, 66.94% in relation to the number of all the obtained candidates (without cutt-offs).

5 Experimental Evaluation and Results

The first evaluation aimed to identify which features must be used for ATE (see Section 3). For that, we applied 2 methods that select attributes by evaluating the attribute subsets. Their evaluation is based on consistency (CBF) and correlation (CFS). We also tested search methods. The combination of these methods, available in WEKA (Hall et al., 2009), is: CFS_SubsetEval using the RankSearch Filter as search method (*CFS_R*), CFS_SubsetEval using the BestFirst as search method (*CFS_BF*), CBF_SubsetEval using the Ranking Filter (*C_R*), and CBF_SubsetEval using the Greedy Stepwise (*C_G*). These methods return feature sets that are considered the most representative for the term classification (Table 2). For the EaD corpus, the *CG* attribute selection method did not select any feature. For our experiments, we also considered all the features (referred by *All*). Additionally, we compared the use of two cut-off types for each feature set, *C1* and *C2*, detailed in Section 4.

For both evaluations[8], we chose largely known inductors in the machine learning area. They represent different learning paradigms: JRip (Rule Induction), Naïve Bayes (Probabilistic), J48 (Decision Tree) with confidence factor of 25%, and SMO (Statistical Learning). All of these algorithms are avail-

Table 2: Features chosen by the attribute selection methods.

Methods	*Corpora*		
	EaD	**ECO**	**N&N**
CFS_R	TFIDF, TV, TVQ, IP, N_Noun, N_Adj	TFIDF, TV, TVQ, POS, N_Noun	Freq, TFIDF, TVQ, IP, Cvalue, N_Noun, POS, N_Adj, N_PO
CFS_BF	Same as in the CFS_R method.	TFIDF, TVQ, TCo, POS	Freq, TFIDF, TV, IP, Cvalue, N_Noun, POS, N_Adj, N_PO
C_R	Freq, DF, TFIDF, TV, TVQ, TCo, IP, GC, POS, FreqGC, NCvalue, Cvalue, N_Adj, N_Noun, N_Verb, N_PO	Freq, DF, TFIDF, TV, TVQ, TCo, GC, Cvalue, NCvalue, IP, S, N_S, POS, N_Noun, N_Adj, N_Verb, N_PO	Freq, DF, TFIDF, TV, TVQ, TCo, GC, IP, S, Cvalue, POS, NCvalue, N_S, N_Noun, N_Adj, N_Verb, N_PO
C_G	Method did not select any feature.	Freq, DF, TFIDF, TV, TVQ, GC, IP, N_S, NCvalue, S, N_Noun, POS, N_Adj, N_PO	Freq, DF, TFIDF, S, TV, TVQ, TCo, IP, NCvalue, N_S, POS, GC, N_Noun, N_PO, N_Verb, N_Adj

able in WEKA and described in (Witten and Frank, 2005). We run the experiments on a 10 fold cross-validation and calculated the precision, recall, and F-measure scores of term classification according to the gold standard of unigrams of each corpus. Using default parameter values for SMO, the results were lower than the other inductors. Due to this fact and the lack of space in the paper, we do not present the SMO results here.

The best precision obtained for the EaD corpus using the term classification, 66.66%, was achieved by the *C_R* attribute selection method with the *C2* cut-off (*C_R-C2*) using the JRIP inductor. The best recall score, 20.96%, was obtained using Naïve Bayes with the *CFS_R-C1* method. The best F-measure was 17.58% using the J48 inductor with *C_R-C2*. For the ECO corpus, the best precision was 60% obtained with the J48 inductor with confidence factor of 25% and the *C_R-C1* method. The best recall was 21.40% with JRIP and the *C_G-C1* method. Our best F-measure was 24.26% obtained with Naïve Bayes using the *CFS_R-C1* method. For the N&N corpus, the best precision score was 61.03% using JRIP. The best recall was 52.53% and the best F-measure score was 54.04%, both using J48 inductor with confidence factor of 25%. The three results used the *All-C2* method.

Table 3 shows the comparison of our best results with 2 baselines, which are the well-known term frequency and TFIDF, using our stoplist. We also considered all the stemmed words of these corpora as CT, except the stopwords, and we calculated the precision, recall, and F-measure scores for these words as well. Finally, we compared our results with the third baseline, which is the only previous work that uniquely extracts unigrams (Zavaglia et al., 2007), described in Section 2. Therefore, this is the state of the art for unigrams extraction for Portuguese. In order to compare this work with our results of the EaD and N&N corpora, we implemented the ATE method of Zavaglia et al. We have to mention that this method uses the normalization technique called lemmatization instead of stemming, which we used in our method. The only difference between our implementation descriptions and the original method is that we POS tagged and lemmatizated the texts using the same parser (PALAVRAS[10] (Bick, 2000)) used in our experiments instead of the MXPOST tagger (Ratnaparkhi, 1996).

For all used corpora, we obtained better results of precision and F-measure comparing with the baselines. In general, we improve the ATE precision scores, for the EaD corpus, eleven times (from 6.1% to 66.66%) and, for the N&N corpus, one and a half times (from 35.4% to 61.03%), both comparing our results with the use of TFIDF. For the ECO corpus, we improve four and a half times (from 12.9% to 60%), by comparing with the use of frequency. We improve the ATE F-measure scores, for the EaD corpus, one and a half times (from 10.93% to 17.58%); for the ECO corpus, we slightly improve the results (from 20.64% to 24.26%); and, for the N&N corpus, two times (from 28.12% to 54.04%). The last three cases are based on the best F-measure values obtained using TFIDF. Regarding recall, on the one hand, the linguistic ExPorTer method (detailed in Section 2), to which we also compare our results, achieved better recall for all used corpora, about 89%. On the other hand, its precision (about 2%) and F-measure (about 4%) were significantly lower than our results.

Finally, if we compare our results with the results of all stemmed words, with the exception of the stopwords, the recall values of the latter are high (about 76%) for all used corpora. However, the precision scores are extremely low (about 1.26%), because it used almost all words of the texts.

[10]As all NLP tools for general domains, PALAVRAS is not excellent for specific domains. However, as it would be expensive (time and manual work) to customize it for each specific domain that we presented in this paper, we decided use it, even though there are error tagging.

Table 3: Comparison with baselines.

Method	*Precision (%)*	*Recall (%)*	*F-Measure (%)*
The EaD corpus			
JRIP with C_R-C2	**66.66**	8.06	14.38
Naïve Bayes with CFS_R-C1	13.19	20.96	16.19
J48 with F.C. of 0.25 with C_R-C2	27.58	12.9	**17.58**
Ling. ExPorTer	0.33	**89.70**	0.66
Hyb. ExPorTer	0.07	17.64	0.15
Frequency	5.9	50.86	10.57
TFIDF	6.1	52.58	10.93
All the corpus	0.52	62.9	1.04
The ECO corpus			
J48 with F.C. of 0.25 with C_R-C1	**60.00**	6.02	10.94
JRIP with C_G-C1	23.44	21.40	22.38
Naïve Bayes with CFS_R-C1	33.33	19.06	**24.26**
Ling. ExPorTer	2.74	**89.18**	5.32
Hyb. ExPorTer	12.76	23.25	16.48
Frequency	12.9	43.28	19.87
TFIDF	13.4	44.96	20.64
All the corpus	1.48	99.07	2.92
The N&N corpus			
JRIP with All-C2	**61.03**	27.73	38.14
J48 with F.C. of 0.25 with All-C2	55.64	52.53	**54.04**
Ling. ExPorTer	3.75	**89.40**	7.20
Hyb. ExPorTer	1.68	35.35	3.22
Frequency	31.6	20.83	25.1
TFIDF	35.4	23.33	28.12
All the corpus	1.83	66.99	3.57

6 Conclusions and Future Work

This paper described ongoing experiments about unigrams extraction using ML. Our first contribution regarding the experiments was to create 4 features and to test 4 features that normally are applied to other tasks and not for automatic term extraction.

Our second contribution is related to the first and fourth ATE problems, which are the existence of silence and noise and low ATE results, respectively. We achieved state of art results for unigrams in Brazilian Portuguese. We improved, for all used corpora, precision (in the best case, we improve the results 11 times using the EaD corpus) and F-measure (in the best case, 2 times using the N&N corpus) and, consequently, we minimized silence and noise.

The third contribution is about the features that are better for extracting domain terms. All the tested attribute selection methods indicated the TFIDF as an essential feature for ATE. 90.9% of the methods selected N_Noun and TVQ, and 81.81% selected TV, IP, N_adj, and POS as relevant features. However, only one of these methods chose Freq_GC, and none of them chose the SG feature. Regarding the levels of knowledge - statistical, linguistic, and hybrid - in which each feature was classified, at least 45.45% of the methods chose 6 statistical, 5 linguistic, and 3 hybrid features. We also observed that the best F-measures (see Tables 2 and 3) were obtained when using at least linguistic and statistical features together. This fact proves that our main hypothesis is true, because we improved the ATE results by joining features of different levels of knowledge. Additionally, we allow the user to choose the features that are better for term extraction.

As the fourth contribution, we minimized the problem of high dimensionality (as mentioned, the second ATE problem) by means of the use of two different cut-offs (*C1* and *C2*). By reducing the number of TCs, fewer candidates were validated or refuted as terms and, consequently, we minimized the third ATE problem, which is the time and human effort for validating the TCs. However, we still perceived the need to reduce more the number of candidates. Therefore, for future work, we intend to use instance selection techniques to reduce the term representation.

We believe to have achieved significant results for the experiments realized to date. Experiments using more features that dependent on general corpus are ongoing. We will also possibly propose new features and will use taxonomic structure in order to improve more the results. For using the taxonomic structure, we intend to create a conventional taxonomy (Miller and Dorre, 1999) is created using the input corpus. Therefore, we may identify more features for the instances considering this taxonomy. For example, normally in a taxonomy's leaf specific words of a domain happen, consequently, terms should appear there. Additionally, we are encouraged to adapt these features for bigram and trigram terms as well.

References

G. M. B. Almeida and O. A. Vale. 2008. Do texto ao termo: interação entre terminologia, morfologia e linguística de corpus na extração semi-automática de termos. In A. N. Isquerdo and M. J. B. Finatto, editors, *As Ciências do Léxico: Lexicologia, Lexicografia e Terminologia*, volume IV, pages 483–499. UFMS, MS, Brazil, 1 edition.

A. Barrón-Cedeño, G. Sierra, P. Drouin, and S. Ananiadou. 2009. An improved automatic term recognition method for spanish. In *Proc of the 10th Int. CNF on Computational Linguistics and Intelligent Text Processing*, pages 125–136, Berlin, Heidelberg. Springer-Verlag.

E. Bick. 2000. *The Parsing System "PALAVRAS". Automatic Grammatical Analysis of Portuguese in a Constraint Grammar Framework*. University of Arhus, Arhus.

M. T. Cabré Castellví, R. Estopà Bagot, and Jordi Vivaldi Palatresi. 2001. Automatic term detection: a review of current systems. In D. Bourigault, C. Jacquemin, and M-C. L'Homme, editors, *Recent Advances in Computational Terminology*, pages 53–88, Amsterdam/Philadelphia. John Benjamins.

J. S. Coleti, D. F. Mattos, L. C. Genoves Junior, A. Candido Junior, A. Di Felippo, G. M. B. Almeida, S. M. Aluísio, and O. N. Oliveira Junior. 2008. *Compilação de Corpus em Língua Portuguesa na área de Nanociência/Nanotecnologia: Problemas e soluções*, volume 1. Tagnin and Vale., SP, Brazil, 192 edition.

J. S. Coleti, D. F. Mattos, and G. M. B. Almeida. 2009. Primeiro dicionário de nanociência e nanotecnologia em língua portuguesa. In Marcelo Fila Pecenin, Valdemir Miotello, and Talita Aparecida Oliveira, editors, *II Encontro Acadêmico de Letras (EALE)*, pages 1–10. Caderno de Resumos do II EALE.

I. Dhillon, J. Kogan, and C. Nicholas. 2003. Feature selection and document clustering. In M. W. Berry, editor, *Survey of Text Mining*, pages 73–100. Springer.

R. Estopà, J. Vivaldi, and M. T. Cabré. 2000. Use of greek and latin forms for term detection. In *Proc of the 2nd on LREC*, pages 855–861, Greece. ELRA.

J. Foo and M. Merkel. 2010. Using machine learning to perform automatic term recognition. In N. Bel, B. Daille, and A. Vasiljevs, editors, *Proc of the 7th LREC - Wksp on Methods for automatic acquisition of Language Resources and their Evaluation Methods*, pages 49–54.

K. T. Frantzi, S. Ananiadou, and J. I. Tsujii. 1998. The C-value/NC-value method of automatic recognition for multi-word terms. In *Proc of the 2nd ECDL*, pages 585–604, London, UK. Springer-Verlag.

A. F. Gelbukh, G. Sidorov, E. Lavin-Villa, and L. Chanona-Hernández. 2010. Automatic term extraction using log-likelihood based comparison with general reference corpus. In *NLDB*, pages 248–255.

A. C. Gianoti and A. Di Felippo. 2011. Extração de conhecimento terminológico no projeto TermiNet. Technical Report NILC-TR-11-01, Instituto de Ciências Matemáticas e de Computação (ICMC) - USP, SP, Brazil.

M. Hall, E. Frank, G. Holmes, B. Pfahringer, P. Reutemann, and I. H. Witten. 2009. The WEKA data mining software: An update. In *SIGKDD-ACM*, volume 11, pages 10–18.

T. Liu, S. Liu, and Z. Chen. 2003. An evaluation on feature selection for text clustering. In *Proceedings of the 10th Int. CNF on Machine Learning*, pages 488–495, San Francisco, CA, USA. Morgan Kaufmann.

L. Liu, J. Kang, J. Yu, and Z. Wang. 2005. A comparative study on unsupervised feature selection methods for text clustering. In *Proc of IEEE NLP-KE*, pages 597–601.

L. Lopes. 2012. *Extração automática de conceitos a partir de textos em língua portugesa*. Ph.D. thesis, Porto Alegre, RS. Pontifícia Universidade do Rio Grande do Sul (PUCRS).

N. Loukachevitch. 2012. Automatic term recognition needs multiple evidence. In N. Calzolari, K. Choukri, T. Declerck, M. Dogan, B. Maegaard, J. Mariani, Odijk, and S. Piperidis, editors, *Proc of the 8th on LREC*, pages 2401–2407, Istanbul, Turkey. ELRA.

A. Miiller and J. Dorre. 1999. The taxgen framework: Automating the generation of a taxonomy for a large document collection. In *Proceedings of the Thirty-Second Annual Hawaii International Conference on System Sciences (HICSS)*, volume 2, pages 2034–2042, Washington, DC, USA. IEEE Computer Society.

R. Nazar. 2011. A statistical approach to term extraction. *Int. Journal of English Studies*, 11(2).

A. Ratnaparkhi. 1996. A maximum entropy model for part-of-speech tagging. *Proc of the CNF on EMNLP*, pages 491–497.

G. Salton and C. Buckley. 1987. Term weighting approaches in automatic text retrieval. Technical report, Ithaca, NY, USA.

J. W. C. Souza and A. Di Felippo. 2010. Um exercício em lingüistica de corpus no âmbito do projeto TermiNet. Technical Report NILC-TR-10-08, ICMC - USP, SP, Brazil.

J. Ventura and J. F. Silva. 2008. Ranking and extraction of relevant single words in text. In Cesare Rossi, editor, *Brain, Vision and AI*, pages 265–284. InTech, Education and Publishing.

J. Vivaldi and H. Rodríguez. 2007. Evaluation of terms and term extraction systems: A practical approach. *Terminology*, 13(2):225–248.

J. Vivaldi, L. A. Cabrera-Diego, G. Sierra, and M. Pozzi. 2012. Using wikipedia to validate the terminology found in a corpus of basic textbooks. In N. Calzolari, K. Choukri, T. Declerck, M. U. Dogan, B. Maegaard, J. Mariani, J. Odijk, and S. Piperidis, editors, *Proc of the 8th Int. CNF on LREC*, Istanbul, Turkey. ELRA.

I. H. Witten and E. Frank. 2005. *Data Mining: Practical Machine Learning Tools and Techniques, Second Edition (Morgan Kaufmann Series in Data Management Systems).* Morgan Kaufmann Publishers Inc., San Francisco, CA, USA.

C. Zavaglia, L. H. M. Oliveira, M. G. V. Nunes, and S. M. Aluísio. 2007. Estrutura ontológica e unidades lexicais: uma aplicação computacional no domínio da ecologia. In *Proc. of the 5th Wksp em Tecnologia da Informação e da Linguagem Humana*, pages 1575–1584, RJ, Brazil. SBC.

Z. Zhang, J. Iria, C. Brewster, and F. Ciravegna. 2008. A comparative evaluation of term recognition algorithms. In N. Calzolari (CNF Chair), K. Choukri, B. Maegaard, J. Mariani, J. Odjik, S. Piperidis, and D. Tapias, editors, *Proc of the 6th on LREC*, pages 2108–2113, Marrakech, Morocco. ELRA.

X. Zhang, Y. Song, and A. Fang. 2010. Term recognition using conditional random fields. In *Proc of IEEE NLP-KE*, pages 333–336.

A Rule-based Approach for Karmina Generation

Franky
Shanghai Jiao Tong University
800 Dongchuan Rd., Shanghai, 200240, China

Charles University in Prague, Faculty of Mathematics and Physics
Malostranské náměstí 25, Prague 1, 11800, Czech Republic

franky.id@gmail.com

Abstract

We present our work in generating Karmina, an old Malay poetic form for Indonesian language. Karmina is a poem with two lines that consists of a hook (*sampiran*) on the first line and a message on the second line. One of the unique aspects of Karmina is in the absence of discourse relation between its hook and message. We approached the problem by generating the hooks and the messages in separate processes using predefined schemas and a manually built knowledge base. The Karminas were produced by randomly pairing the messages with the hooks, subject to the constraints imposed on the rhymes and on the structure similarity. Syllabifications were performed on the cue words of the hooks and messages to ensure the generated pairs have matching rhymes. We were able to generate a number of positive examples while still leaving room for improvement, particularly in the generation of the messages, which currently are still limited, and in filtering the negative results.

1 Introduction

Computational creativity is an interesting area of research, since it deals with how a machine can actually produce something new and creative. Creative, in the sense that it is something that usually comes from human's imagination, which is quite abstract, and unexpected from a machine. In this work, we investigated the matter of creativity in language. In particular, we focused our work in the generation of Karmina, an old Malay poetic form for Indonesian language.

Karmina is a poem that consists of two lines with around 8-12 syllables on each line. The first line is called the hook, which acts as the opening line of the poem. The second line is called the message, which contains the meaning of the poem. The language used in Karmina is usually less formal, i.e. closer to conversational language. Karmina resembles *Pantun,* a more well-known form of Malay poetic form, but is different from Pantun in the number of lines it has. It can probably be compared to a couplet in English, in terms of the number of lines and rhymes it must follows. Due to its short presentation, Karmina is also called a *quick* Pantun.

One of the unique aspects of Karmina is in its hook and message relationship. The hook on the first line has no discourse relation with the message on the second line. Take as an example Karmina presented below in Indonesian:

*Gendang gend**ut** tali kecap**i***
*Kenyang per**ut** senanglah hat**i***
(Fat drum string of lute
Full stomach makes a happy heart)

and also our attempt to make one in English:

*Soft meat**ball** is easy to **chew***
*Love them **all** but trust a **few***

The hook in Karmina acts as the entrance of the poem and is used to engage interest or curiosity of the audience. It usually talks about something common in daily life, some unusual or less mean-

Proceedings of the NAACL HLT 2013 Student Research Workshop, pages 24–31,
Atlanta, Georgia, 13 June 2013. ©2013 Association for Computational Linguistics

ingful information, or obvious facts, e.g. *Buah pisang warnanya kuning* (Banana is yellow).

The message of Karmina contains the real meaning that wants to be delivered by the author. It might contain ideas, jokes, mockeries, or even advices. The sentence used in the message does not need to be formal. It creates its poetic form by omitting some function words, changing the word order, or by using the base form of the word instead of using a morphologically derived one.

The rhyme scheme in Karmina is formally deemed to be *a-a*. But we found that most of the Karminas have the rhyme schemes of (*a b*)-(*a b*), with (*a b)* in the same line, as shown in the examples above. The position of the rhyme *a* in an (*a b*) line is usually located in the middle of the sentence and is determined by how to read the Karmina so that the rhymes on both lines match to each other.

We chose to work with Karmina due to its simple and short presentation. It will be both challenging and interesting to answer the question of whether we can computationally generate a simple and short poem that contains a single idea (meaning), while at the same time maintain its poetic characteristics. From a cultural point of view, we considered this as one of the ways to conserve this poem, as well as to introduce it to others.

We centered our work in generating Karmina with rhyme schemes of (*a b*)-(*a b*). We considered Karmina in this form to be more poetic and have more interesting structure. We present our work by first mentioning some related works in the area of poetry generation in Section 2. In Section 3, we describe our approach for syllabification, hook and message generation, and the construction of the final Karmina. We present the results of our experiments in Section 4. The discussions of findings, issues, and future works are presented in Section 5.

2 Related Works

Some recent works in poetry generation are in the area of English Haiku generation. In Netzer et al. (2009), the authors use word association information to enrich user supplied seed words with their associated words. Candidate lines are produced from pre-extracted lines that match the seed words and their associated words, as well as the chosen syntactic patterns. The poems are generated by random line matching processes and by filtering the generated Haikus based on some constraints and internal associativity scores. The work by Wong and Chun (2008) uses a different approach. They represent the extracted line as a vector of words. The Haikus are produced by generating sentence pairs based on the selected seed words. They are then ranked based on the similarity scores of their lines.

Other previous work in a more general area of poetry is by Manurung et al. (2000). In this work, they proposed a stochastic hill climbing search model that iteratively produces set of candidate solutions and evaluates them based on some defined phonetic, linguistic, and semantic measures. Gervas (2001) and Díaz-agudo et al. (2002) focus their works in the area of Spanish poetry generation. They use prose description and rough specification from user as their input. The appropriate strophic forms are selected based on this input. The process continues using a case based reasoning approach to produce the final poem.

We consider our work to have different focus and pose different challenges. The first thing is that the meaning of a Karmina can be understood directly. This property might be different from other type of poetry which requires deeper interpretation. Hence, the problem usually lies in generating a poem with a deep embedded meaning. The second one is related to the property of the hook that should contain less important information (ignorable) compared to the message. We believe that we could fulfill these two requirements by defining proper schemas and constraints, and by controlling the words used. The last thing to consider is about the absence of discourse relation between the hook and the message. Our current approach to the problem is by generating the hooks and the messages separately using different knowledge base and different constraints. By this treatment, we expect the generated hooks and messages to be independent of each other.

3 Our Current Approach

In his thesis, Manurung (2003) defines three properties that a poem should fulfill: meaningfulness, grammaticality, and poeticness. We think that these three are inherent properties of Karmina and unquestionably should be fulfilled by the generated poem. Meaningfulness is handled by putting constraints on the proposed schemas which restrict the words used in the poem. It is also supported by ensuring the grammaticality of the poem, which is handled by positioning the words inside the schema properly. In terms of poeticness, we consider that Karmina obtains its poeticness through its rhyme structure, limitation on the number of words or syllables, and the forms of the words used. Hence, poeticness is handled by considering these three aspects in the generation of the poem.

We will start this section with the description of the schemas used in generating the hooks and the messages. We will then continue with the explanation of the syllabification algorithm and the generation of the Karmina.

3.1 Generating the Hook

The hook of Karmina can be recognized from its characteristic of somehow sounds like an 'unimportant' utterance, e.g. *kelapa diparut enak rasanya* (*grated coconut tastes good*) or *ikan lele beli di pasar* (*catfish bought from the market*). In our first attempt, we took text segments from the collections of news, blogs, and reviews websites. The segments were produced by splitting the sentences using punctuations, such as comma, period, question mark, single and double quotes, and exclamation mark. We were hoping to find segments that could be used as hooks. But, we found that this kind of utterance is quite rare.

We looked deeper into some of the examples of Karmina and found something interesting. The majority of the hooks that we met have some similar syntactic and semantic patterns. We analyzed the examples and came out with a set of schemas to generate the hooks. One property of Karmina that we think makes the generation of the hook possible is that a sentence in Karmina usually consists of only 4-5 words. We defined around 19 schemas for the hook. Some of them differ only in their word order, e.g. a sentence with a word order of `X Y Z` and a sentence with a word order of `X Z Y`, where `X`, `Y`, `Z` can be noun, verb, adjective, etc. These schemas are not exhaustive. They cover some of the hooks that we found on our small examples. Other forms of hooks may also present.

The knowledge base was built manually by finding all suitable nouns, verbs, and other necessary information. We did some categorization on them, e.g. as fish, flower, tree, location, and specified their relations as required in the schemas. We describe in this section the first three schemas that we defined. We use "," (comma) to denote a conjunction and ";" (semicolon) to denote a disjunction.

`Schema 1`

Dahulu `X` *sekarang* `Y`

`Constraints`

`Noun(X), Noun(Y), ChangeTo(X,Y),`
`Length(X,1), Length (Y,1)`

In **`Schema 1`**, the generated hook will have a meaning of *before* (*dahulu*) and *after/now* (*sekarang*). In this case, `X` and `Y` are usually replaced by nouns that have this kind of relationship. The replacement using other word classes is also possible. We restricted `X` and `Y` to noun since it is the most common class we saw on the examples. In order to check for this relationship, we defined a predicate `ChangeTo` that check for two things from the knowledge base:

- Whether `X` can be made from `Y` and vice versa, e.g. knife is made from iron.
- Whether `X` is better than `Y` and vice versa, e.g. gold is better than silver.

Predicate `Length` checks for how many words the noun `X` and `Y` has, which we limit to 1, to maintain the poeticness of the generated hook. In our current work, we used the number of words instead of syllables to simplify the word selection process, with the assumption that the number of syllables inside a word is around two to four syllables.

`Schema 2`

Sudah `X Y` *pula*

`Constraints`

`Noun(X), Noun(Y), SameType(X,Y),`
`Length(X,1), Length(Y,1), (Tree(X);`
`Flower(X); Food(X))`

`Schema 2` was made from one of the examples that we found. The `X` and `Y` come from the same category, i.e. both are the name of fish, bird, vegetable, island, tree, etc. The meaning of the generated hook will be that `Y` is redundant because `X` is already present. We restricted `X` and `Y` to be in the same category to give an emphasis on this redundancy. We used tree, flower, and food for the categories. This was based on our experiments that using other categories resulted in a sentence with odd meaning.

```
Schema 3
  X Propnya Y
Constraints
  Noun(X), Adjective(Y), Has(X, Prop,
  Y) Length(X,2), Length(Y,1)
```

In **`Schema 3`**, the generated hook simply means `X` with a property `Prop` that has the value of `Y`. For example, `X` can be a banana (*buah pisang*) with a property of color (*warna*) and property's value of yellow (*kuning*). Hence, the generated hook will be *Buah pisang warnanya kuning* (Banana has a yellow color). We found that this kind of hook is quite often used.

3.2 Generating the Message

The message of Karmina is more free in its meaning and structure. Creating all possible schemas is not a feasible option. However, we managed to find messages that follow certain schemas. They have the same structures with the **`Schema 1`** and **`Schema 2`**. Hence, in this work, the message was generated by using these two schemas only. These two schemas bind the hook and the message to have the same structure, i.e. both have the structures of *Dahulu* `X` *sekarang* `Y` or *Sudah* `X` `Y` *pula*. They differ in the types and constraints of the `X` and `Y` used. We experimented using a list of positive and negative sentiment words to replace `X` and `Y`.

For **`Schema 1`**, `X` and `Y` were replaced by words that have different sentiment (positive-negative or negative-positive). These two words are antonym to each other. The generated message will have a meaning of a change from a positive (good) to negative (bad) condition, or vice versa, e.g. *Dahulu kaya sekarang miskin* (was rich but now poor).

In **`Schema 2`**, `X` and `Y` were replaced by words that have the same sentiment. We expected the resulting sentences to contain the repetition of two good or two bad expressions and hence, intensifying the positive or negative condition. For example, *Sudah busuk bau pula* (rotten and stink).

To our knowledge, there are no subjectivity lexicons for Indonesian. Hence, we produced the list by translating English subjectivity lexicon (Hu and Liu, 2004), which originally has 2006 positive words and 4783 negative words, using Google Translate. The translation results were then filtered manually to remove untranslated words, bad translations, and words that do not contain positive or negative sentiment. The final lexicon contains 740 positive words and 1500 negative words.

3.3 Syllabification

The syllabification is used in searching for the hooks that rhyme with the messages. We used a set of rules to cut syllables out of the word iteratively. The syllabification starts from the front and by looking into the pattern of the first 3-6 letters of the word. We defined rules for the possible patterns that determine how many letters from the front that will be taken as a syllable. The syllable is cut out from the word and the iteration continues with the truncated word. The iteration stops when only two or less letters are left. The patterns are the combinations of vowel-consonant patterns and alphabet letters. The vowel-consonant pattern is simply a sequence of *v* (vowel) and *c* (consonant) marker. There are only five vowels in Indonesian (*a,i,u,e,o*).

```
kecapi (cvcvcv) (take first 2)
capi   (cvcv)   (take first 2)
pi     (cv)     (take all)
```

Figure 1. Syllabification of *kecapi* to (*ke, ca, pi*)

The example in Figure 1 shows the word *kecapi* matches the `cvcv` pattern, and the rule specifies to take the first two letters from the front (`ke`) as a syllable. The truncated word *capi* also falls into the same rule. In the last step, only two letters are left and we took them all as a syllable.

3.4 Rhymes

In our work, we used two types of rhymes, perfect and imperfect (half). In Indonesian, the pronunciation of a word can be determined from its syllables and hence, we can check whether two words rhyme with each other by matching their last syllables. For perfect rhyme, we considered two words as having perfect rhyme if they have the same last syllables. For imperfect rhyme, we divided the case into two. If the last letter of the last syllable is a vowel, we took this vowel to be compared. If the last letter is a consonant, we searched for the first vowel from the last after the consonant and took the vowel together with the following consonants to be compared. For diphthong (*ai, au, oi*), we took both of the vowels to be compared.

3.5 Constructing the Karmina

The Karmina was produced by first generating a list of hooks and a list of messages. The generation processes were done separately for the hook and the message. We selected one of the messages and we tried to find a proper hook for the message from the list of hooks.

Syllabifications were performed on the cue words of the selected message and on the cue words of the hooks in the list. Cue words of hook or message are the middle word and the last word of the sentence. Given the schema, we can usually determine the second word as the middle word.

We produced a list of possible hooks for the selected message by selecting hooks that rhyme with the message, producing *(a b)-(a b)* rhyme scheme. It was done by comparing the last syllables of the cue words of the message and the hooks. We differentiated the hooks which have perfect rhymes with the message and the hooks which have imperfect rhymes. We gave higher priority to the hooks that rhyme perfectly with the message. If no such hooks exist, we took the hook from the later.

Message generated using **`Schema 1`** or **`Schema 2`** could only take the hook that has the same structure. Hence, in this work, the generated Karmina could only have the structure of **`Schema 1`** or **`Schema 2`** on both of its lines.

The final Karmina was produced by pairing the selected message with one of the possible hooks which was selected randomly from the list.

4 Experiments

We implemented our work for syllabification and Karmina construction in Perl, and generation of the hooks and the messages in Prolog. We evaluated the syllabification on a small list of 258 unique words taken from two news articles. We found that 16 words were incorrectly syllabified. The main causes are due to incomplete rules, foreign words or abbreviations, and ambiguous words. Examples of ambiguous words are *beribu* that can be read as *ber-ibu* or *be-ribu*, and words that contain diphthong-like string such as ***bai**kan* and *bag**ai**kan*. In the first word, the *ai* is not a diphthong. Both cases might require context disambiguation and lemmatization which are not covered in the current rule-based syllabification.

For Karmina evaluation, first we generated lists of all possible hooks and messages from **`Schema 1`** and **`Schema 2`**. Next, we generated all possible Karminas from these lists. However, we found that all generated Karminas were in the form of **`Schema 2`**. We failed to generate Karmina for **`Schema 1`** since there were no hooks and messages that rhyme with each other due to small number of hooks and messages that we have for **`Schema 1`**. Table 1 shows the evaluation results.

Table 1. Karmina Evaluation

Hook	Message	Total
Proper	Proper	10
Proper	Not Proper	30
Not Proper	Proper	1
Not Proper	Not Proper	59
		100

The evaluation was performed on 100 randomly selected Karminas. The proper and improper annotations were done through discussions by two native speakers. We managed to get 10 Karminas with acceptable hooks and messages. We found that the improper hook was mainly caused by the use of uncommon names e.g. *holdi*, *hamboi*. The other cause was that **`X`** and **`Y`** in **`Schema 2`** may sometimes not be able to be placed side by side, e.g. *Sudah tomat srikaya pula* (tomato and sugar-apple). Although both of the objects are fruits, the more common perception of tomato is as vegetables and hence, the sentence sounds strange.

a) Sudah leci menteng pula (lychees and menteng)
Sudah ahli tampan pula (skilled and handsome)

b) Sudah kiwi ceri pula (cherry and kiwi)
Sudah ahli kejujuran pula (skilled and honesty)

Figure 2. (a) Positive example (b) Negative example

For the message, the main cause was as shown in Figure 2 (b). The sentence sounds unusual because it combines adjective *skilled* with noun *honesty*. This happened because of the incomplete constraints on the schema, i.e. no restriction in the part of speech of `X` and `Y`. Other reason was because of words that do not fit to be put together, e.g. *Sudah agung bagus pula* (majestic and smart).

5 Discussion and Future Works

In this section, we discuss several findings and issues that we found, and our future plans for the work.

Incomplete Constraints. The constraints in the schema are the most crucial parts of the generation process. The grammaticality, meaning, and poeticness of the generated sentence depend on the constraints used. Hence, some of the problems as the one shown in Figure 2 were caused by incomplete specification of the constraints.

Manual Intervention. The main issue in utilizing knowledge base and schemas is in the amount of manual work that needs to be performed in creating them. One of the problems is in the information collection, such as collecting property of nouns (e.g. skin as property of a fish and the skin of a fish is slippery), antonyms, and what kind of verb that can match certain noun (e.g. coconut can be grated). Currently, the information was built manually and hence slowly.

One of the options to automate the knowledge creation such as 'what *object* has what kind of *property* with what *value*' is by first generating all possible combinations of nouns and properties, and finding a way to validate this knowledge efficiently. Data that contains this information might be needed for validation. Another option might be to query a search engine. Using collocation information in the results, we may somehow validate the knowledge. However, the policy of automated query of current search engine might be a hurdle.

The other issue is if we want to automate the creation of the schema. Using extracted sentences and part of speech information may be useful. But this approach might not be enough, since we also need to capture the dependency between items. Without deeper constraints, the extracted schema will be just a shallow representation.

Filtering the Knowledge. We found that having too much knowledge about certain things can actually result in a less or non-poetic sentence, e.g. a hook *kod pasifik kulitnya licin* (pacific cod has slippery skin). Grammatically and semantically, there is nothing wrong with the sentence. The problem lies in the use of *kod pasifik* (pacific cod) that is rarely mentioned in a normal daily life. Since the hook is usually about something common to the majority of the audience, using a rare term like this might cause it to lose its poeticness.

Corpus Based Approach for Message Generation. We are considering the corpus-based approach that utilizes the segments extracted from the corpus for message generation. Contrary to the hook, we found that the use of segments for the message is more promising. We experimented with blog corpus, since we considered it as the most proper corpus, because of its informal and conversational style language. We picked segments that have length (number of words) greater than two, and for poeticness reason, do not start with certain function words. The chosen segments were further processed by normalizing slang words, e.g. *gw* to *saya*. Further removal of unpoetic function words (*yang, adalah, untuk*) was performed. The final segments that have length more than three were stored. The Karmina generation was performed using the same procedure. We determined the middle word of the message by taking the word where the fourth syllable is located. Figure 3 shows the positive examples that we were able to generate. One important aspect that we still need to consider is about the characteristics of the segments that can be considered as good messages.

Ikan cakalang di danau emas	(tuna in lake emas)
Selamat ulang tahun ya mas	(happy birthday)
Sungai bengkulu sungai bilah	(bengkulu and bilah river)
Aku malu kepada allah	(i am ashamed of god)

Figure 3. Positive examples of Karmina using corpus based approach for message part

6 Conclusions

We described our work in Karmina generation that utilized a rule-based approach in generating the hooks and the messages. We considered the notion of grammaticality, meaningfulness, and poeticness by defining proper schemas and constraints. We also discussed some of the problems and future improvements in section 5. We concluded that the rule-based approach is able to produce some positive examples. Some limitations still exist, especially in the message generation, and a lot of improvements are still needed to produce more of proper Karmina. We are considering the corpus-based approach in our future work for the message generation and a more automated approach in knowledge collection.

References

B. Díaz-agudo , P. Gervás, and P.A. González-calero. 2002. Poetry Generation in COLIBRI. *Advances in Case-Based Reasoning* (2002): 157-159.

H.M. Manurung, G. Ritchie, and H. Thompson. 2000. Towards a computational model of poetry generation.In *Proc. of the AISB'00*.

H.M. Manurung. 2003. An evolutionary algorithm approach to poetry generation. Ph.D. thesis, University of Edinburgh.

J. M. Toivanen, H.Toivonen, A.Valitutti, and O. Gross 2012. Corpus-based generation of content and form in poetry. In *International Conference on Computational Creativity, Dublin, Ireland* (pp. 175-179).

M. Hu and B. Liu. 2004. Mining and Summarizing Customer Reviews. In *Proceedings of the ACM SIGKDD International Conference on Knowledge Discovery and Data Mining (KDD-2004)*.

M. Tsan Wong and A. Hon Wai Chun. 2008. Automatic Haiku generation using VSM. In *Proc. of ACACOS'08*, April.

N. Tosa, H. Obara, and M. Minoh. 2008. Hitch haiku: An interactive supporting system for composing haiku poem. In *Proc. of the 7th International Conference on Entertainment Computing*.

P. Gervas. 2001. An expert system for the composition of formal Spanish poetry. *Journal of Knowledge-Based Systems*, 14.

P. Gervas. 2002. Exploring quantitative evaluations of the creativity of automatic poets. In *Proc. of the 2nd Workshop on Creative Systems, Approaches to Creativity in Artificial Intelligence and Cognitive Science, the 15th European Conf. on Artificial Intelligence (ECAI 2002)*.

Y. Netzer, D.Gabay, Y.Goldberg, and M.Elhadad. 2009. Gaiku: generating Haiku with word associations norms. In *Proceedings of the Workshop on Computational Approaches to Linguistic Creativity*.

Appendix A. Schemas for Hook Generation

The rest of the schemas used for generating the hooks are provided below as references. Some additional relations that might need to be explained are:

- `Location(X)`: `X` is a location, e.g. name of a mountain, name of a river, etc.
- `LocationType(X)`: location type of `X`, e.g. `X` is a river, a mountain, or other abstract types such as on the top of an object (*on a table*), inside an object, etc.
- `Has(X,Y,A,B)`: `Y` is performed on `X`, resulting in `X` with property `A` and property value of `B`, e.g. `Has(fish, fried, taste, good).`

We use Prolog notations such as "," (comma) to denote a conjunction, ";" (semicolon) to denote a disjunction, and "_" (underscore) to denote any matching term.

Schema 4

Sudah ke X *ke* Y *pula*

Constraints

```
Location(X), Location(Y), Location-
Type(X)==LocationType(Y),
Length(X,1), Length (Y,1)
```

Schema 5

X Y Prop*nya*

Constraints

```
Noun(X), Adjective(Y), Has(X,Prop,Y)
Length(X,2), Length(Y,1)
```

Schema 6

X *di*Z Y Prop*nya*

Constraints

```
Noun(X), Verb(Z), Adjective(Y),
Has(X,Z,Prop,Y)
```

Schema 7

X *di*Z Prop*nya* Y

Constraints

```
Noun(X), Verb(Z), Adjective(Y),
Has(X,Z,Prop,Y)
```

Schema 8

X Z *di* Y

Constraints

```
Noun(X), Verb(Z), Location(Y),
not(Location(X)), Has(X,Z,_,_),
Length(X,1)
```

Schema 9

X *di* Y

Constraints

```
Noun(X), Location(Y),
not(Location(X)), Length(X,2),
Length(Y,2)
```

Schema 10

X Y

Constraints

Noun(X), Noun(Y), SameType(X,Y), Length(X,2), Length(Y,2)

Schema 11

X X Y Y

Constraints

Noun(X), Noun(Y), SameType(X,Y), Length(X,1), Length(Y,1)

Schema 12

X Y Y

Constraints

Noun(X), Noun(Y), SameType(X,Y), Length(X,2), Length(Y,1)

Schema 13

X X Y

Constraints

Noun(X), Noun(Y), SameType(X,Y), Length(X,1), Length(Y,2)

Schema 14

X Y A A

Constraints

Noun(X), Adjective(Y), Noun(A), Has(X,_,Y), SameType(X,A), Length(X,1), Length(A,1)

Schema 15

X Y A B

Constraints

Noun(X), Adjective(Y), Noun(A), Adjective(B), Has(X,_,Y), Has(A,_,B), Length(X,1), Length(A,1)

Schema 16

X Y A

Constraints

Noun(X), Adjective(Y), Noun(A), Has(X,_,Y), SameType(X,A), Length(X,1), Length(A,2)

Schema 17

X A B

Constraints

Noun(X), Noun(A), Adjective(B), Has(A,_,B), SameType(X,A), Length(X,2), Length(A,1)

Schema 18

X Z Y Prop*nya*

Constraints

Noun(X), Verb(Z), Adjective(Y), Has(X,Z,Prop,Y)

Schema 19

X Z Prop*nya* Y

Constraints

Noun(X), Verb(Z), Adjective(Y), Has(X,Z,Prop,Y)

From Language to Family and Back: Native Language and Language Family Identification from English Text

Ariel Stoleman **Aylin Caliskan Islam** **Rachel Greenstadt**
Dept. of Computer Science
Drexel University
Philadelphia, PA
{ams573,ac993,greenie}@cs.drexel.edu

Abstract

Revealing an anonymous author's traits from text is a well-researched area. In this paper we aim to identify the native language and language family of a non-native English author, given his/her English writings. We extract features from the text based on prior work, and extend or modify it to construct different feature sets, and use support vector machines for classification. We show that native language identification accuracy can be improved by up to 6.43% for a 9-class task, depending on the feature set, by introducing a novel method to incorporate language family information. In addition we show that introducing grammar-based features improves accuracy of both native language and language family identification.

1 Introduction

Mining text for features to infer characteristics on its author is an important research field. One author property that has been researched is native language, extracted from the author's writing in a non-native language. Learning the native language of an anonymous author can assist in profiling criminals or terrorists, and may also undermine the privacy of legitimate anonymous authors by helping to unveil their identity.

Influences of native language (L1) on second language (L2), referred as the L1-L2 transfer effect, is seen in writing and can be utilized to identify native language. In this paper we examine aspects of a broader class – the language family to which the native language of an author belongs. In the rest of the paper native language and native language family will be referred as L1 and LF, respectively.

First, we examine the correct classification rates of LF compared to L1. As L1 is a subset of LF, the number of L1 classes is greater than or equal to the number of corresponding LF classes. Therefore, higher LF classification accuracy can be achieved trivially by taking the family of the attributed L1 in a L1 classification task. This can be helpful in cases where high accuracy is preferred over resolution. We introduce a novel, improved method that achieves higher correct classification rate for LF identification, compared to the trivial method.

Our main contribution is showing that L1 identification accuracy can be increased by incorporating family information via LF identification.

We use stylometric analysis and machine learning techniques to identify L1 and LF. We conduct a series of experiments by mining English text written by non-native English authors for linguistic features. We use 4 different feature sets detailed in section 3. We evaluate the accuracy of our results by examining the true-positive rate.

The novelty of our work is in exploring the LF-L2 transfer effect using stylometric methods, and expanding L1 identification methods accordingly. Increasing the state-of-the-art correct classification rate for L1 detection is not our main goal. Instead, we introduce concepts to increase achieved accuracy by incorporating LF knowledge into the classification process.

The next section (2) provides background and prior work. Section 3 describes the experimental setup. In section 4 we describe the different experiments that were performed, followed by results and evaluation. We finalize with discussion on the given results (section 5), followed by conclusions and directions for future research (section 6).

2 Related Work

Literature includes work on extracting demographic and psychological traits from different data formats, such as speech and text samples. Native language and accent identification from speech can be found

Proceedings of the NAACL HLT 2013 Student Research Workshop, pages 32–39,
Atlanta, Georgia, 13 June 2013.

in (Choueiter et al., 2008; Tomokiyo and Jones, 2001). Identifying an author's native language from L2 text, which is English in most cases, is the closest problem to our work.

Introductory studies in the area identified the written or spoken language itself, focusing on telephone dialogue corpora (Ahmed et al., 2004; Zissman, 1993). Further studies focused on extracting specific information from text or speech after identifying the language being used. Wanneroy et al. (1999) investigated how non-native speech deteriorated language identification and used acoustic adaptation to improve it. Choueiter et al. (2008) classified different foreign accented English speech samples by using a combination of heteroscedastic LDA and maximum mutual information training. Tomokiyo and Jones (2001) characterized part-of-speech sequences and showed that Naïve Bayes classification can be used to identify non-native utterances of English.

The first work that utilized stylometric methods for native language attribution is introduced by Koppel et al. (2005a; 2005b). They explored frequencies of sets of features, and used them with multi-linear support vector machines to classify text by author's native language. They used a set of features consisted of function words, letter n-grams, errors and idiosyncrasies, and experimented on a dataset of authors of five different native languages taken from ICLEv1 (Granger et al., 2002), reaching to 80.2% accuracy. Tsur and Rappoport (2007) revisited Koppel's work using only the 200 most frequent character bigrams, and achieved 65.6% accuracy, with only a small degradation when removing dominant words or function words.

Brooke and Hirst (2012) presented a method of utilizing native language corpora for identifying native language in non-native texts. They used word-by-word translation of large native language corpora to create sets of second language forms that are possible results of language transfer, later used in unsupervised classification. They achieved results above random chance for L1 identification, however insufficiently accurate.

More related work can be found in (Estival et al., 2007; van Halteren, 2008; Carrio-Pastor, 2009; Golcher and Reznicek, 2009; Wong and Dras, 2009; Wong et al., 2011; Brooke and Hirst, 2011; Ahn, 2011). The work mentioned above and our approach both utilize the L1-L2 transfer effect to gain information about an author's native language. Gibbons (2009) proved the impact of native language family's typological properties on L2. As far as we know, our work is the first to combine stylometry and native language family's effect on L2, utilized for L1 identification.

3 Experimental Setting

3.1 Corpus

We use the ICLEv2 (Granger et al., 2009) corpus that contains English documents written by intermediate to advanced international learners of English, with language backgrounds of 16 mother-tongues. The first version of the corpus was used in significant previous work (Koppel et al., 2005a; Koppel et al., 2005b; Tsur and Rappoport, 2007). They reported that they were able to use 258 documents of sizes 500-1000 words for each language they used. We use version 2 of the corpus and restrict all documents in our experiments to those with 500-1000 words as well. However, we found that constraining our documents to these lengths allows us to use only 133-146 documents per language. We conduct a series of experiments with different sub-corpora constructed of documents representing 11 native languages out of the 16 available in the corpus. The native languages we used are: Bulgarian, Czech, Dutch, French, German, Italian, Norwegian, Polish, Russian, Spanish and Swedish, all Indo-European languages. These languages represent 3 language-families in a coarse partition: Germanic, Slavic and Romance, which are used as the LF class in the experiments to follow. All sub-corpora configurations are detailed in section 4.

Since we are looking at a set of languages from both L1 and LF aspects, we maintained only the sub-corpora that allowed a sufficient amount of languages in each represented family, i.e. 3 languages in each of the Germanic, Slavic and Romance families. Therefore we removed 5 of the 16 available languages in the corpus.

3.2 Feature Selection

Koppel et al. represented each document in their experiment as a 1,035-dimensional feature vector: 400 function words, 200 most frequent letter n-grams, 185 misspellings and syntactic errors and 250 rare POS bigrams. The 250 rare POS bigrams are the least common bigrams extracted from the Brown Corpus (Francis and Kucera, 1983), and their appearances are considered to be erroneous or non-standard.

In our experiments we used 4 different feature sets, partially based on that used by Koppel et al. We used the authorship attribution tool JStylo (McDonald et al., 2012) for feature extraction. The feature sets are the following:

Basic: includes the 400 most frequent function words, 200 most frequent letter bigrams, 250 rare POS bigrams and 300 most frequent spelling errors.

The 400 most frequent function words were taken from a list of 512 function words used in the original experiments by Koppel et al. For the 200 letter n-grams, we chose bigrams, as they are shown to be effective for the task in previous research. The 250 rare POS bigrams were extracted from the Brown Corpus using the POS tagger in (Toutanova et al., 2003). Finally, we simplified the error types by considering only misspelled words, based on a list of 5,753 common misspellings, constructed from Wikipedia common misspellings and those used in (Abbasi and Chen, 2008). We ignored any misspellings with 0-1 appearances across the entire sub-corpus. Since many of the rare POS bigrams and misspellings had no appearances, the effective vector lengths vary between 653-870 features.

Extended: identical to the former, with the addition of the 200 most frequent POS bigrams across the entire sub-corpus used for each experiment. These syntactic features were selected as an additional representation of grammatical structures in the text.

There are several methods for natural language classification, including genetic, typological and areal (Campbell and Poser, 2008). We consider the typological classification that uses structural features to compare similarities between languages and classify them into families. Therefore we chose grammatical evidence in L2 as features that may represent similar transfer effects among languages in the same family.

Grammatical: constructed only from the 200 most frequent POS bigrams, representing the grammatical level of the text.

InfoGain: We used the 200 features with the highest information gain extracted from the extended feature set using Weka (Hall et al., 2009), calculated for any given feature by measuring the expected reduction in entropy caused by partitioning the test instances according to that feature.

3.3 Classification

We trained a SMO (Platt, 1998) SVM classifier with polynomial kernel, chosen as SVMs are used extensively in prior work and ours outperformed other methods tested, including decision trees, nearest-neighbors, Bayesian and logistic regression classifiers.

4 Experimental Variations and Evaluation

We conducted 3 different experiments using various sub-corpora and the 4 feature sets described in the previous sections, with L1 and LF classification tasks. We evaluated the results by using the true-positive rate to capture accuracy. Following is a detailed description of the different variations and results.

4.1 9-Class Languages, 3-Class Families

Setup: We compared 9-L1 identification with the corresponding 3-LF identification, using datasets constructed of the sub-corpus containing all 11 languages mentioned before. For the 9-L1 task we randomly sampled documents of 9 languages, 3 for each of the Germanic, Slavic and Romance language families, in order to maintain the same number of languages per family in every experiment. We constructed 16 different 9-L1 sets, choosing 3 out of 4 Germanic languages, 3 out of 4 Slavic languages and the only 3 Romance languages available. In each of the 16 experiments we used the same number of documents per language, varying between 133-146.

In order to compare results with LF identification, we conducted 3 sets of experiments, each containing 16 3-LF experiments, corresponding to the 16 that were performed for L1 identification.

First, we ran the trivial experiment of attributing the family of the predicted language resulted from the L1 identification experiments. This method is denoted as the *trivial* method.

Next, we ran the same experiments conducted for L1, with the only difference of using LF as the class rather than L1. As a result of that configuration, each experiment also contained the same number of documents per language family, varying between 399-438. This method is denoted as the *standalone* method (as it is a standalone experiment, independent of L1 classification results).

Lastly, we ran experiments combining the standalone and trivial approaches. We hypothesize that if L1 is attributed with high confidence, so is the LF of that attributed L1, however if the confidence level decreases, a standalone LF experiment achieves better results. We ran the L1 identification experiments and set a threshold as the averaged probability of the predicted class across the entire test set, based on the class probability distribution outputted by the SVM classifier. To obtain proper probability estimates, we fit logistic regression models to the outputs of the SVM. Every instance classified with probability above the threshold was attributed the family using the trivial method, and every instance below – using the standalone method. This method is denoted as the *combined* method.

Results: We averaged the results of all 16 L1 identification experiments, and those of the 3 sets of 16 LF identification experiments. See figure 1.

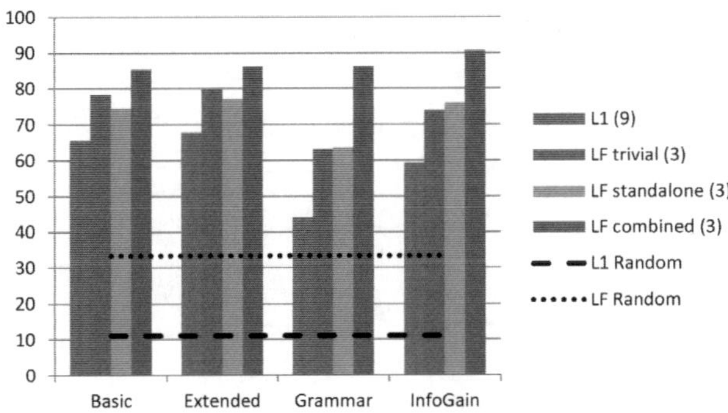

Figure 1: Accuracy for 9-class L1 and 3-class LF identification. The combined method for LF outperforms the other two.

The accuracy for L1 identification was 67.78%, 65.64%, 59.34% and 44.02% for the extended, basic, InfoGain and grammatical feature sets, respectively.

Out of the 3 LF identification experiment sets, the combined method achieved the best accuracy: 90.57%, 86.24%, 86.2% and 85.29% for the InfoGain, grammatical, extended and basic feature sets, respectively. These results support our hypothesis.

The trivial method achieved better results than the standalone method for the basic and extended feature sets: 78.33% and 79.87% for the first, 74.53% and 77.24% for the latter. For the grammatical and InfoGain feature sets, the standalone performed better than the trivial: 63.61% and 76.02% for the first, 63.1% and 73.94% for the latter.

Since the L1 identification experiments have more classes than the LF experiments, the random chance varies between them: 11.11% for L1 and 33.33% for LF. Although the absolute accuracy for LF is consistently higher than for L1, if we subtract the corresponding random chance values to obtain *"effective"* accuracy, in most cases L1 is more accurate than LF. The LF combined method is the only one out of the 3 LF methods that exceeds the effective accuracy of L1, for the grammatical and InfoGain feature sets. Combined with the standard (non-effective) results, it appears that the InfoGain feature set with the LF combined method achieves the highest accuracy with the most added knowledge over random classification, across all tasks and feature sets. It is also notable that the smallest difference between L1 and LF identification accuracy is seen for the grammatical feature set. See figure 2.

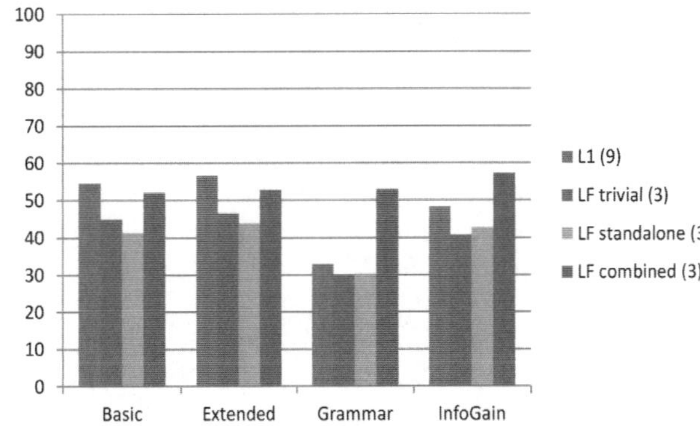

Figure 2: Effective accuracy for 9-L1 and 3-LF identification. Accuracy for L1 exceeds most accuracy results for LF, except for the combined method on the grammatical and InfoGain feature sets.

4.2 3-Class Languages, 3-Class Families

Setup: In order to have the same random-chance baseline for both L1 and LF tasks, we compared 3-L1 with 3-LF identification, using the same subcorpus as before.

For L1 we constructed 9 experiments, in each randomly sampling 3 languages from 1, 2 and 3 different language families (3 experiments each). The reason for this choice is that as more families are used, the farther the chosen languages are from one another. Therefore the choice above is intended to balance the effect of LF in those experiments. We used 133 documents per language for all experiments.

For LF we constructed 2 sets of 9 experiments, in order to examine the notion that languages in the same family have more family-distinguishable commonalities as opposed to random sets of languages. In the first, for each of the experiments we randomly created 3 sets of languages to be considered as families. We randomly sampled documents from all 11 languages to construct sets for the 3 randomly-generated families used as classes. Here we also maintained 133 documents per language family. In the second we ran a similar configuration, only using the actual language families.

Results: The averaged accuracy for L1 was 84.23%, 82.29%, 81.67% and 66.97% for the extended, InfoGain, basic and grammatical feature sets, respectively. These results consistently outperformed the results of both sets of LF experiments. See figure 3.

The accuracy attained for actual language families

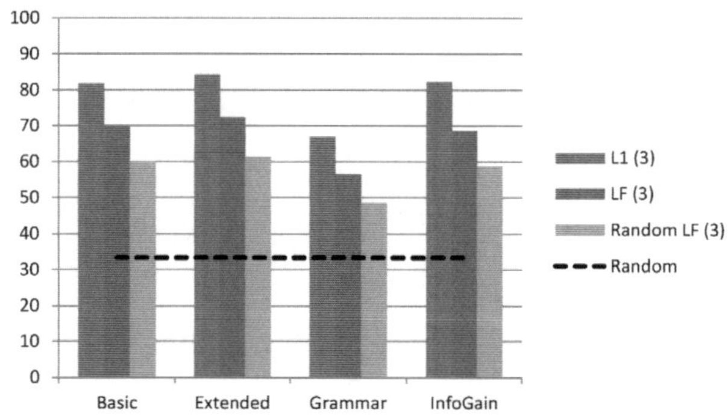

Figure 3: Accuracy for 3-L1, 3-LF and 3-randomly-generated families identification. Using the original families achieves the highest accuracy for LF identification.

was 72.43%, 70.09%, 68.72% and 56.55% for the extended, basic, InfoGain and grammatical feature sets, respectively, which consistently outperformed that of the randomly-generated families: 61.46%, 60.01%, 58.81% and 48.67%. This shows that partitioning the languages into sets by their actual family achieves the highest accuracy for LF identification. As in the previous experiment, the difference in accuracy between L1 and LF identification was the smallest with the grammatical feature set.

4.3 9-Class Languages, Reclassify by Family

Setup: We wanted to examine whether LF classification can improve L1 classification. In this experiment we conducted the same 16 9-L1 experiments from section 4.1. We then set a threshold as in the *combined* method in section 4.1, such that each classified instance with predicted probability less than that threshold is treated as misclassified. For all allegedly-misclassified instances we attributed the family they belong to, using various methods detailed later. As last step we reclassified those instances using a training set constructed only of the 3 languages in the family they were classified as, and considered these results as L1 classification-correction for those instances. We measured the overall change in accuracy.

The entire 16 10-fold cross-validation experiments were conducted 3 times, each with a different method for LF attribution for the instances below the threshold: 1) The standalone method – running LF identification task over all those instances, using the same training set (with families as classes rather than languages), 2) The trivial method – using the family of the predicted language of those instances, and 3) Random – randomly selecting the family.

Results: We averaged the results of all 16 L1 experiments for each of the 3 LF attribution methods and each of the 4 feature sets used.

We measured the net fix in accuracy (added number of correctly classified instances, taking into account corrected classifications and new misclassifications). For all feature sets, LF attribution using the standalone method yielded the highest fix rate, followed by LF attribution using the trivial method. The randomly attributed family method consistently yielded negative fix rate (i.e. reduced overall accuracy). See figure 4.

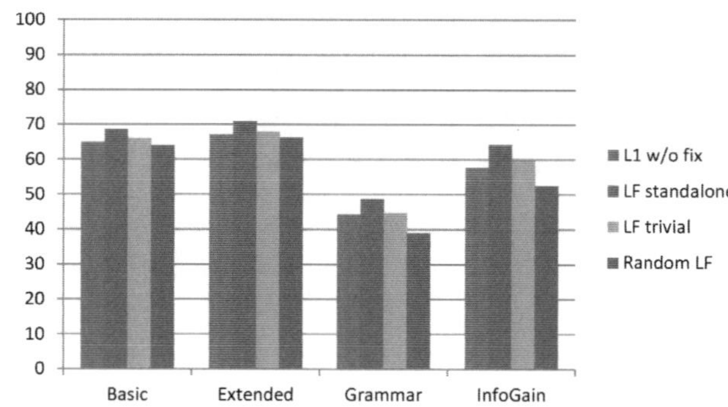

Figure 4: Accuracy for L1 identification without fix and with fixing using LF attribution by the standalone method, trivial method and random selection of family. The standalone method yields the highest net fix in L1 classification accuracy.

The extended feature set yielded the best results. Starting at a baseline of 67.17% for L1 identification without any fix, the true-positive rates obtained for this feature set were 70.9% and 68.05% for attributing LF by the standalone and the trivial methods, respectively. The increase in accuracy is statistically significant ($p < 0.01$). The random family attribution method yielded a decrease in accuracy to 66.35%.

It is notable that although yielding best results for the extended feature set, the standalone method achieved higher increase in accuracy in some of the other feature sets. The increase rates for this method were: 6.43%, 4.48%, 3.73% and 3.67% for the InfoGain, grammatical, extended and basic feature sets, respectively.

5 Discussion

The first notable result is seen in experiment 4.1, where using the combined method for LF identification derives higher accuracy than both the trivial and the standalone methods. This may suggest that when L1 is predicted with high confidence, LF is predicted well, but when the confidence level is low, it is better to run standalone LF classification. Since the combined method uses the best of the two others, it outperforms both.

The most important result is seen in experiment 4.3, where L1 identification is improved by up to 6.43% in accuracy for 9-L1 classification by introducing information about the language family, thus providing a smaller set of language classes in which the actual language is more likely to be found. Attributing LF by standalone experiments yielded higher L1 classification accuracy than attributing it by the family of the predicted language. This outcome seemingly contradicts the results seen in section 4.1, where the latter LF attribution method outperformed the first. However, this only supports the idea suggested above regarding the threshold, that the family of the attributed L1 is the actual family with higher probability than LF attributed by a standalone experiment, only when L1 is attributed with high confidence (i.e. above the selected threshold).

The results in sections 4.1 and 4.2 suggest that all 4 feature sets achieve better accuracy for L1 than for LF (standalone) classification. We believe this is since for L1 we try to distinguish between individual languages as they transfer to English. However, LF identification necessitates finding features that intersect between languages in a particular family, and distinguish well between different families as they are transferred to English. This makes LF identification a more difficult task.

The results obtained for randomly generated families in sections 4.2 and 4.3, which are consistently lower than using the actual families, suggest that the contribution of using the latter yields the best performance. That is, languages in the same family have more commonalities distinguishing them from other families, than random sets of languages have.

Looking at the results using the different feature sets, in most cases the extended feature set outperformed the rest. This shows that adding grammatical features increases accuracy for both L1 and LF. Furthermore, in all experiments using *only* the grammatical features achieved a rather good accuracy (significantly higher than random chance), considering that we used only 200 of these features. This supports the notion that grammatical features are useful for both L1 and LF identification.

Another interesting notion regarding the grammatical feature set is seen in the portion these features consist of the InfoGain feature set for the experiments of section 4.2: 33.05% for L1 and 57.16% for LF. This suggests that the grammatical level of the text has greater significance for identifying LF compared to L1. When analyzing the portion lexical features consist of the InfoGain feature set, an opposite trend is seen: function words and letter bigrams consist 29.94% and 33.94% of the features for L1, as opposed to 17.44% and 23.55% for LF, respectively. This suggests that the lexical level of the text is better for L1 detection than for LF detection. Although less significant, the same trend is seen with spelling errors: 3% for L1 and 1.83% for LF.

6 Conclusion

The main conclusion is that when trying to gain information about the native language of an English text author, integrating family identification can increase the total accuracy, using the method introduced in section 4.3, where all low-confidence classifications are reapplied within a smaller set of candidates – languages within the family attributed to those instances using a standalone experiment.

Furthermore, when dealing with a large number of L1 classes, higher accuracy can be attained by reducing the level of specification to language families, which can be obtained with high accuracy using the combined method presented in this paper that integrates both the trivial LF by predicted L1 and LF by standalone experiment methods using the average confidence level as threshold.

In addition, using the most frequent POS bigrams, which represent the grammatical level of the text, is shown to increase accuracy in both L1 and LF identification tasks, especially for the latter. Using lexical features as function words and character bigrams is helpful especially for L1 identification.

We suggest several directions for future work. First, trying new feature sets that may capture other similarities between languages in the same family. For instance, since languages in the same family tend to share basic vocabulary, it may have some level of transfer to L2 that could be captured by a synonym-based classifier. For instance, "verde" in Spanish and "vert" in French may be translated to "verdant", whereas "grün" in German and "groen" in Dutch may be translated to "green".

In addition, we can further explore the notion of increasing accuracy by applying knowledge of a broader class on the task applied in other stylometry-based information extraction tasks. For instance, using wide age ranges as the broader class for classifying age of anonymous authors, or personality prototypes for personality type identification.

References

Ahmed Abbasi and Hsinchun Chen. 2008. Writeprints: A stylometric approach to identity-level identification and similarity detection in cyberspace. *ACM Trans. Inf. Syst.*, 26(2):7:1–7:29, April.

Bashir Ahmed, Sung-Hyuk Cha, and Charles Tappert. 2004. Language identification from text using n-gram based cumulative frequency addition. Proc. CSIS Research Day, May.

Charles S. Ahn. 2011. Automatically detecting authors' native language. Thesis, Naval Postgraduate School, March.

Julian Brooke and Graeme Hirst. 2011. Native language detection with 'cheap' learner corpora. In *The 2011 Conference of Learner Corpus Research (LCR2011)*.

Julian Brooke and Graeme Hirst. 2012. Measuring interlanguage: Native language identification with l1-influence metrics. In Nicoletta Calzolari (Conference Chair), Khalid Choukri, Thierry Declerck, Mehmet Ugur Dogan, Bente Maegaard, Joseph Mariani, Jan Odijk, and Stelios Piperidis, editors, *Proceedings of the Eight International Conference on Language Resources and Evaluation (LREC'12)*, Istanbul, Turkey, may. European Language Resources Association (ELRA).

Lyle Campbell and William J. Poser. 2008. *Language Classification: History and Method*. Cambridge University Press.

Maria Luisa Carrio-Pastor. 2009. Contrasting specific english corpora: Language variation. *International Journal of English Studies, Special Issue*, pages 221–233.

Ghinwa F. Choueiter, Geoffrey Zweig, and Patrick Nguyen. 2008. An empirical study of automatic accent classification. In *ICASSP*, pages 4265–4268.

Dominique Estival, Tanja Gaustad, Son B. Pham, Will Radford, and Ben Hutchinson. 2007. Author profiling for english emails. In *10th Conference of the Pacific Association for Computational Linguistics (PACLING 2007)*, pages 262–272.

Winthrop Nelson Francis and Henry Kucera. 1983. *Frequency Analysis of English Usage: Lexicon and Grammar*. Houghton Mifflin.

Erin Elizabeth Gibbons. 2009. The effects of second language experience on typologically similar and dissimilar third language. Thesis, Brigham Young University, Center for Language Studies.

Felix Golcher and Marc Reznicek. 2009. Stylometry and the interplay of topic and l1 in the different annotation layers in the falko corpus. In *Humboldt-Universitat zu Berlin*, QITL-4. [Online: Stand 2012-03-22T16:09:09Z].

Sylvaine Granger, Estelle Dagneaux, and Fanny Meunier. 2002. *International Corpus of Learner English : Version 1 ; Handbook and CD-ROM*. Pr. Univ. de Louvain, Louvain-la-Neuve.

Sylvaine Granger, Estelle Dagneaux, Magali Paquot, and Fanny Meunier. 2009. *The International Corpus of Learner English, Version 2: Handbook and CD-Rom*. Pr. Univ. de Louvain, Louvain-la-Neuve.

Mark Hall, Eibe Frank, Geoffrey Holmes, Bernhard Pfahringer, Peter Reutemann, and Ian H. Witten. 2009. The weka data mining software: an update. *SIGKDD Explor. Newsl.*, 11(1):10–18, November.

Moshe Koppel, Jonathan Schler, and Kfir Zigdon. 2005a. Automatically determining an anonymous author's native language. In *Proceedings of the 2005 IEEE international conference on Intelligence and Security Informatics*, ISI'05, pages 209–217, Berlin, Heidelberg. Springer-Verlag.

Moshe Koppel, Jonathan Schler, and Kfir Zigdon. 2005b. Determining an author's native language by mining a text for errors. In *Proceedings of the eleventh ACM SIGKDD international conference on Knowledge discovery in data mining*, KDD '05, pages 624–628, New York, NY, USA. ACM.

Andrew McDonald, Sadia Afroz, Aylin Caliskan, Ariel Stolerman, and Rachel Greenstadt. 2012. Use fewer instances of the letter "i": Toward writing style anonymization. July.

J. Platt. 1998. Fast training of support vector machines using sequential minimal optimization. In B. Schoelkopf, C. Burges, and A. Smola, editors, *Advances in Kernel Methods - Support Vector Learning*. MIT Press.

Laura Mayfield Tomokiyo and Rosie Jones. 2001. You're not from 'round here, are you?: naive bayes detection of non-native utterance text. In *Proceedings of the second meeting of the North American Chapter of the Association for Computational Linguistics on Language technologies*, NAACL '01, pages 1–8, Stroudsburg, PA, USA. Association for Computational Linguistics.

Kristina Toutanova, Dan Klein, Christopher Manning, and Yoram Singer. 2003. Feature-rich part-of-speech tagging with a cyclic dependency network. In *Human Language Technology Conference (HLT-NAACL 2003)*.

Oren Tsur and Ari Rappoport. 2007. Using classifier features for studying the effect of native language on the choice of written second language words. In *Proceedings of the Workshop on Cognitive Aspects of Computational Language Acquisition*, CACLA '07, pages 9–16, Stroudsburg, PA, USA. Association for Computational Linguistics.

Hans van Halteren. 2008. Source language markers in europarl translations. In *Proceedings of the 22nd International Conference on Computational Linguistics - Volume 1*, COLING '08, pages 937–944, Stroudsburg, PA, USA. Association for Computational Linguistics.

R. Wanneroy, E. Bilinski, C. Barras, M. Adda-Decker, and E. Geoffrois. 1999. Acoustic-phonetic modeling of non-native speech for language identification. In *Proceedings of the ESCA-NATO Workshop on Multi-Lingual Interoperability in Speech Technology (MIST)*, The Netherlands.

Sze-Meng Jojo Wong and Mark Dras. 2009. Contrastive analysis and native language identification. In *Proceedings of the Australasian Language Technology Association Workshop 2009*, pages 53–61, Sydney, Australia, December.

Sze-Meng Jojo Wong, Mark Dras, and Mark Johnson. 2011. Topic modeling for native language identification. In *Proceedings of the Australasian Language Technology Association Workshop 2011*, pages 115–124, Canberra, Australia, December.

Marc A. Zissman. 1993. Automatic language identification using gaussian mixture and hidden markov models. In *Proceedings of the 1993 IEEE international conference on Acoustics, speech, and signal processing: speech processing - Volume II*, ICASSP'93, pages 399–402, Washington, DC, USA. IEEE Computer Society.

Ontology Label Translation

Mihael Arcan and Paul Buitelaar

Unit for Natural Language Processing,
Digital Enterprise Research Institute (DERI)
National University of Ireland Galway (NUIG)
Galway, Ireland

{mihael.arcan , paul.buitelaar}@deri.org

Abstract

Our research investigates the translation of ontology labels, which has applications in multilingual knowledge access. Ontologies are often defined only in one language, mostly English. To enable knowledge access across languages, such monolingual ontologies need to be translated into other languages. The primary challenge in ontology label translation is the lack of context, which makes this task rather different than document translation. The core objective therefore, is to provide statistical machine translation (SMT) systems with additional context information. In our approach, we first extend standard SMT by enhancing a translation model with context information that keeps track of surrounding words for each translation. We compute a semantic similarity between the phrase pair context vector from the parallel corpus and a vector of noun phrases that occur in surrounding ontology labels. We applied our approach to the translation of a financial ontology, translating from English to German, using Europarl as parallel corpus. This experiment showed that our approach can provide a slight improvement over standard SMT for this task, without exploiting any additional domain-specific resources.

1 Introduction

The biggest barrier for EU-wide cross-lingual business intelligence is the large number of various languages used by banks or investment firms for their financial reports. In contrast to that, most of the ontologies used for knowledge access are available in English, e.g. the financial ontology FINREP[1] (FINancial REPorting) or COREP[2] (COmmon solvency ratio REPorting). To make the targeted transparency of financial information possible, these ontologies have to be translated first into another language; see also (Declerck et al., 2010). The challenge here lies in translating domain-specific ontology vocabulary, e.g. *Equity-equivalent partner loans*, *Subordinated capital* or *Write-downs of long-term financial assets and securities*.

Since domain-specific parallel corpora for SMT are hardly available, we used a large general parallel corpus, whereby a translation model built by such a resource will tend to translate a segment into the most common word sense. This can be seen for instance when we translate the financial ontology label *Equity-equivalent partner loans* from the German GAAP ontology (cf. Section 3.1). Using a baseline SMT system we get the translation *Gerechtigkeit-gleichwertige Partner Darlehen*. Although this label provides contextual information, *equity* is translated into its general meaning, i.e. *Gerechtigkeit* in the meaning of *justice*, *righteousness* or *fairness*, although *Eigenkapital* would be the preferred translation in the financial domain.

To achieve accurate disambiguation we developed a method using context vectors. We extract semantic information from the ontology, i.e. the vocabulary and relations between labels and compare it with the contextual information extracted from a parallel corpus.

The remainder of the paper is organized as fol-

[1] http://eba.europa.eu/Supervisory-Reporting/FINER.aspx
[2] http://eba.europa.eu/Supervisory-Reporting/COREP.aspx

Proceedings of the NAACL HLT 2013 Student Research Workshop, pages 40–46,
Atlanta, Georgia, 13 June 2013. ©2013 Association for Computational Linguistics

lows. Section 2 gives an overview of the related work on including semantic information into SMT. Section 3 describes the ontology and the parallel corpus used in our experiment. Then we describe the approach of enhancing the standard SMT model with ontological knowledge for improving the translation of labels in Section 4. In Section 5 the results of exploiting the ontological knowledge described in the previous section are illustrated. Finally we conclude our findings and give an outlook for further research.

2 Related Work

Word sense disambiguation (WSD) systems generally perform on the word level, for an input word they generate the most probable meaning. On the other hand, state of the art translation systems operate on sequences of words. This discrepancy between unigrams versus n-grams was first described in (Carpuat and Wu, 2005). Likewise, (Apidianaki et al., 2012) use a WSD classifier to generate a probability distribution of phrase pairs and to build a local language model. They show that the classifier does not only improve the translation of ambiguous words, but also the translation of neighbour words. We investigate this discrepancy as part of our research in enriching the ontology label translation with ontological information. Similar to their work we incorporate the idea of enriching the translation model with neighbour words information, whereby we extend the window to 5-grams.

(Mauser et al., 2009) generate a lexicon that predicts the bag of output words from the bag of input words. In their research, no alignment between input and output words is used, words are chosen based on the input context. The word predictions of the input sentences are considered as an additional feature that is used in the decoding process. This feature defines a new probability score that favours the translation hypothesis containing words, which were predicted by the lexicon model. Similarly, (Patry and Langlais, 2011) train a model by translating a bag-of-words. In contrast to their work, our approach uses bag-of-word information to enrich the missing contextual information that arises from translating ontology labels in isolation.

(McCrae et al., 2011) exploit in their research the ontology structure for translation of ontologies and taxonomies. They compare the structure of the monolingual ontology to the structure of already translated multilingual ontologies, where the source and target labels are used for the disambiguation process of phrase pairs. We incorporated the idea of using the ontology structure, but avoided the drawback of exploiting existing domain-specific multilingual ontologies.

3 Data sets

For our experiment we used a general parallel corpus to generate the mandatory SMT phrase table and language model. Further, the corpus was used to generate feature vectors on the basis of the contextual information provided by surrounding words. Finally we calculate the semantic similarity between the extracted information from the parallel corpus and the ontology vocabulary.

3.1 Financial ontology

For our experiment we used the financial ontology German GAAP (Generally Accepted Accounting Practice),[3] which holds 2794 concepts with labels in German and English.

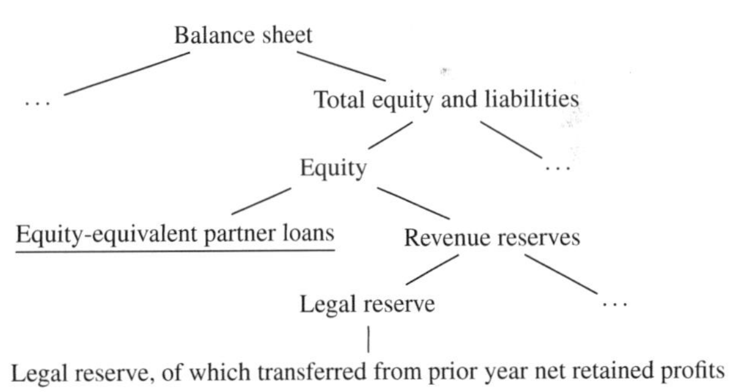

Figure 1: The financial label *Equity-equivalent partner loans* and its neighbours in the German GAAP ontology

As seen in Figure 1 the financial labels do not correspond to phrases from a linguistic point of view. They are used in financial or accounting reports as unique financial expressions or identifiers to organise and retrieve the reported information automatically. Therefore it is important to translate these financial labels with exact meaning preservation.

[3]http://www.xbrl.de/

3.2 Europarl

As a baseline approach we used the Europarl parallel corpus,[4] which holds proceedings of the European Parliament in 21 European languages. We used the English-German parallel corpus with around 1.9 million aligned sentences and 40 million English and 43 million German tokens (Koehn, 2005).

Although previous research showed that a translation model built by using a general parallel corpus cannot be used for domain-specific vocabulary translation (Wu et al., 2008), we decided to train a baseline translation model on this general corpus to illustrate any improvement steps gained by enriching the standard approach with the semantic information of the ontology vocabulary and structure.

4 Experiment

Since ontology labels (or label segments) translated by the Moses toolkit (Section 4.1) do not have much contextual information, we addressed this lack of information and generated fromthe Europarl corpus a new resource with contextual information of surrounding words as feature vectors (Section 4.2). A similar approach was done with the ontology structure and vocabulary (Section 4.3).

4.1 Moses toolkit

To translate the English financial labels into German, we used the statistical translation toolkit Moses (Koehn et al., 2007), where the word alignments were built with the GIZA++ toolkit (Och and Ney, 2003). The SRILM toolkit (Stolcke, 2002) was used to build the 5-gram language model.

4.2 Building the contextual-semantic resource from the parallel corpus Europarl

To enhance the baseline approach with additional semantic information, we built a new resource of contextual information from Europarl.

From the original phrase table, which was generated from the Europarl corpus, we used the sub-phrase table, which was generated to translate the German GAAP financial ontology in the baseline approach. Although this sub-phrase table holds only segments necessary to translate the financial labels, it still contains 2,394,513 phrase pairs. Due to the scalability issue, we reduced the number of phrase pairs by filtering the sub-phrase table based on the following criteria:

a) the direct phrase translation probability $\phi(e|f)$ has to be larger than 0.0001

b) a phrase pair should not start or end with a functional word, i.e. prepositions, conjunctions, modal verbs, pronouns

c) a phrase pair should not start with punctuation

After applying these criteria to the sub-phrase table, the new filtered phrase table holds 53,283 entities, where phrase pairs, e.g. *tax rate ||| Steuersatz* or *tax liabilities ||| Steuerschulden* were preserved.

In the next step, the phrase pairs stored in the filtered phrase table were used to find sentences in Europarl, where these phrase pairs appear. The goal was to extract the surrounding words as the contextual information of these phrase pairs. If a segment from the filtered phrase table appeared in the sentence we extracted the lemmatised contextual information of the phrase pair, whereby we considered 10 tokens to the left and 10 to the right of the analysed phrase pair. To address the problem of different inflected forms (*financial asset* vs. *financial assets*) of the same lexical entity (*financial asset*) we lemmatised the English part of the Europarl corpus with TreeTagger(Schmid, 1995). Similar to the phrase table filtering approach, an n-gram should not start with a functional word or punctuation. The extracted surrounding words were stored together with its phrase pairs, i.e. for the phrase pairs *Equity-Gerechtigkeit* and *Equity-Eigenkapital* different contextual vectors were generated.

Example 1.a) illustrates a sentence, which holds the source segment *Equity* from the filtered phrase table. Example 1.b) represents its translation into German. This example illustrates the context in which *Equity* is translated into the German expression *Gerechtigkeit*. The segment *Equity* is also present in the second sentence, (example 2.a)), in contrast to the first one, *equity* is translated into *Eigenkapital*, (2.b)), since the sentence reports financial information.

1. a) ... which could guarantee a high standard of efficiency, safety and **equity** for employees and users alike, right away.

[4] http://www.statmt.org/europarl/, version 7

b) ... , der heute ein hohes Niveau an Leistung, Qualität, Sicherheit und **Gerechtigkeit** für die Bediensteten und die Nutzer garantieren könnte.

2. a) ... or organisations from making any finance, such as loans or **equity**, available to named Burmese state-owned enterprises.

   b) ... bzw. Organisationen zu verbieten, birmanischen staatlichen Unternehmen jegliche Finanzmittel wie Darlehen oder **Eigenkapital** zur Verfügung zu stellen.

Applying this methodology on all 1.9 million sentences in Europarl, we generated a resource with feature vectors for all phrase pairs of the filtered phrase table. Table 1 illustrates the contextual differences between the vectors for *Equity-Gerechtigkeit* and *Equity-Eigenkapital* phrase pairs.

4.3 Contextual-semantic resource generation for the financial ontology German GAAP

To compare the contextual information extracted from Europarl a similar approach was applied to the vocabulary in the German GAAP ontology.

First, to avoid unnecessary segments, e.g. *provisions for* or *losses from executory*, we parsed the financial ontology with the Stanford parser (Klein and Manning, 2003) and extracted meaningful segments from the ontology labels. This step was done primarily to avoid comparing all possible n-gram segments with the filtered segments extracted from the Europarl corpus (cf. Subsection 4.2). With the syntactical information given by the Stanford parser we extracted a set of noun segments for the ontology labels, which we defined by the rules shown in Table 2.

#	Syntactic Patterns
1	(NN(S) w+)
2	(NP (NN(S) w+)+))
3	(NP (JJ w+)+ (NN(S) w+)+))
4	(NP (NN(S) w+)+ (CC w+) (NN(S) w+)+)
5	(NP (NN(S) w+)+ (PP (IN/.. w+) (NP (NN(S) w+)+))

Table 2: Syntactic patterns for extracting noun segments from the parsed financial ontology labels

Applying these patterns to the ontology label *Provisions for expected losses from executory contracts* extracts the following noun segments: *provisions*, *losses* and *contracts* (pattern 1), *expected losses* and *executory contracts* (pattern 3), *provisions for expected losses* and *expected losses from executory contracts* (pattern 5).

In the next step, for all 2794 labels from the financial ontology, a unique contextual vector was generated as follows: for the label *Equity-equivalent partner loans* (cf. Figure 1), the vector holds the extracted (lemmatised) noun segments of the direct parent, *Equity*, and all its siblings in the ontology, e.g. *Revenue reserves* ... (Table 3).

targeted label:	Equity-equivalent partner loans
contextual information:	capital (6), reserve (3), loss (3), balance sheet (2) ... currency translation (1), negative consolidation difference (1), profit (1)

Table 3: Contextual information for the financial label *Equity-equivalent partner loans*

4.4 Calculating the Semantic Similarity

Using the resources described in the previous sections in a final step we apply the Cosine, Jaccard and Dice similarity measures on these feature vectors.

For the first evaluation step we translated all financial labels with the general translation model. Table 4 illustrates the translation of the financial expression *equity* as part of the label *Equity-equivalent partner loans*.[5]

With the n-best (n=50) translations for each financial label we calculated the semantic similarity between the contextual information of the phrase pairs (*equity-Eigenkapital*) extracted from the parallel corpus (cf. Table 1) with the semantic information of the financial label *Equity* extracted from the ontology (cf. Table 3).

After calculating a semantic similarity, we reorder the translations based on this additional information, which can be seen in Table 5.

[5] ger. Gerechtigkeit-gleichwertige Partner Darlehen

Source label	Target label	$p(e\|f)$
equity	Gerechtigkeit	-10.6227
equity	Gleichheit	-11.5476
equity	Eigenkapital	-12.7612
equity	Gleichbehandlung	-13.0936
equity	Fairness	-13.6301

Table 4: Top five translations and its translation probabilities generated by the Europarl translation model

Source label	Target label	Context (frequency)
equity	Gerechtigkeit	social (19), efficiency (18), efficiency and equity (14), justice (13), social equity (11), education (9), principle (8), transparency (7), training (7), great (7)
equity	Eigenkapital	capital (19), equity capital (15), venture (3), venture capital (3), rule (2), capital and risk (2), equity capital and risk (2), bank (2), risk (2), debt (1)

Table 1: Contextual information for *Equity* with its target labels *Gerechtigkeit* and *Eigenkapital* extracted from the Europarl corpus

Source label	Target label	Jaccard
equity	Eigenkapital	0.0780169232
equity	Equity	0.0358268041
equity	Kapitalbeteiligung	0.0341965597
equity	Gleichheit	0.0273327211
equity	Gerechtigkeit	0.0266209669

Table 5: Top five re-ranked translations after calculating the Jaccard similarity

5 Evaluation

Our evaluation was conducted on the translations generated by the baseline approach, using only Europarl, and the ontology-enhanced translations of financial labels.

We undertook an automatic evaluation using the BLEU (Papineni et al., 2002), NIST (Doddington, 2002), TER (Snover et al., 2006), and Meteor[6] (Denkowski and Lavie, 2011) algorithms.

5.1 Baseline Evaluation of general corpus

At the beginning of our experiment, we translated the financial labels with the Moses Toolkit, where the translation model was generated from the English-German Europarl aligned corpus. The results are shown in Table 7 as *baseline*.

5.2 Baseline Evaluation of filtered general corpus

A second evaluation on translations was done on a filtered Europarl corpus, depending if a sentence holds the vocabulary of the ontology to be translated. We generated five training sets, based on n-grams of the ontology vocabulary (from unigram to 5-gram) appearing in the sentence. From the set of aligned sentences we generated new translation models and translated again the financial ontology labels with them. Table 6 illustrates the results of filtering the Europarl parallel corpus into smaller (n-gram) training sets, whereby no training set outperforms significantly the baseline approach.

model	sentences	BLEU-4	Meteor	OOV
baseline	1920209	4.22	0.1138	37
unigram	1591520	4.25	0.1144	37
bigram	322607	4.22	0.1077	46
3-gram	76775	1.99	0.0932	92
4-gram	4380	2.45	0.0825	296
5-gram	259	0.69	0.0460	743

Table 6: Evaluation results for the filtered Europarl baseline translation model (OOV - out of vocabulary)

5.3 Evaluation of the knowledge enhanced general translation model

The final part of our research concentrated on translations where the general translation model was enhanced with ontological knowledge. Table 7 illustrates the results using the different similarity measures, i.e. Dice, Jaccard, Cosine similarity coefficient.

For the Cosine coefficient we performed two approaches. For the first step we used only binary values (bv) from the vector, where in the second approach we used the frequencies of the contextual information as real values (rv). The results show that the Cosine measure using frequencies (rv) performs best for the METEOR metric. On the other hand the binary Cosine measure (bv) performs better than the other metrics in BLEU-2 and NIST metrics.

The Jaccard and Dice similarity coefficient perform very similar. They both outperform the general translation model in BLEU, NIST and TER metrics, whereby the Jaccard coefficient performs slightly better than the Dice coefficient. On the other hand both measures perform worse on the METEOR metric regarding the general model. Overall we observe that the Jaccard coefficient outperforms the baseline

[6]Meteor configuration: -l de, exact, stem, paraphrase

	Bleu-2	Bleu-4	NIST	Meteor	TER
baseline	13.05	4.22	1.789	0.113	1.113
Dice	13.16	4.43	1.800	0.111	1.075
Jaccard	13.17	**4.44**	1.802	0.111	**1.074**
Cosine (rv)	12.91	4.20	1.783	**0.117**	1.108
Cosine (bv)	**13.27**	4.34	**1.825**	0.116	1.077

Table 7: Evaluation results for Europarl baseline translation model and the different similarity measures

approach by 0.22 BLEU points.

5.4 Comparison of translations provided by the general model and Jaccard similarity

Table 7 illustrates the different approaches that were performed in our research. As the automatic metrics give just a slight intuition about the improvements of the different approaches, we compared the translations of the general translation model manually with the translations on which Jaccard similarity coefficient was performed.

As discussed, *Equity* can be translated into German as *Gerechtigkeit* when translating it in a general domain or into *Eigenkapital* when translating it in the financial domain. In the financial ontology, the segment *Equity* appears 126 times. The general translation model translates it wrongly as *Gerechtigkeit*, whereby the Jaccard coefficient, with the help of contextual information, favours the preferred translation *Eigenkapital*. Furthermore *Equit* can be also part of a larger financial label, e.g. *Equity-equivalent partner loans*, but the general translation model still translates it into *Gerechtigkeit*. This can be explained by the segmentation during the decoding process, i.e. the SMT system tokenises this label into separate tokens and translates each token separately from each other. On the contrary, the Jaccard similarity coefficient corrects the unigram segment to *Eigenkapital*.

As part of the label *Uncalled unpaid contributions to subscribed capital (deducted from equity on the face of the balance sheet)*, *equity* is again translated by the general translation model as *Gerechtigkeit*. In this case the Jaccard coefficient cannot correct the translation, which is caused by the general model itself, since in all n-best (n=50) translations *equity* is translated as *Gerechtigkeit*. In this case the Jaccard coefficient reordering does not have any affect.

The manual analysis further showed that the ambiguous ontology label *Securities*, e.g. in *Write-downs of long-term financial assets and securities* was also often translated as *Sicherheiten*[7] in the meaning of *certainties* or *safeties*, but was corrected by the Jaccard coefficient into *Wertpapiere*, which is the correct translation in the financial domain.

Finally, the analysis showed that the segment *Balance* in *Central bank balances* was often translated by the baseline model into *Gleichgewichte*,[8] i.e. *Zentralbank Gleichgewichte*, whereas the Jaccard coefficient favoured the preferred translation *Guthaben*, i.e. *Zentralbank Bankguthaben*.

Conclusion and Future Work

Our approach to re-using existing resources showed slight improvements in the translation quality of the financial vocabulary. Although the contextual information favoured correct translations in the financial domain, we see a need for more research on the contextual information stored in the parallel corpus and also in the ontology. Also more work has to be done on analysis of the overlap of the contextual information and the ontology vocabulary, e.g. which contextual words should have more weight for the similarity measure. Furthermore, dealing with the ontology structure, the relations between the labels, i.e. part-of and parent-child relations, have to be considered. Once these questions are answered, the next step will be to compare the classical cosine measure against more sophisticated similarity measures, i.e. Explicit Semantic Analysis (ESA) (Gabrilovich and Markovitch, 2007). Instead of measuring similarity between the vectors directly using cosine, we will investigate the application of ESA to calculate the similarities between short texts by taking their linguistic variations into account (Aggarwal et al., 2012).

Acknowledgments

This work is supported in part by the European Union under Grant No. 248458 for the Monnet project and Grant No. 296277 for the EuroSentiment project as well as by the Science Foundation Ireland under Grant No. SFI/08/CE/I1380 (Lion-2).

[7] ger. Abschreibungen der langfristigen finanziellen Vermögenswerte und Sicherheiten

[8] en. *equilibrium, equation, balance*

References

Aggarwal, N., Asooja, K., and Buitelaar, P. (2012). DERI&UPM: Pushing corpus based relatedness to similarity: Shared task system description. In *SemEval-2012*.

Apidianaki, M., Wisniewski, G., Sokolov, A., Max, A., and Yvon, F. (2012). Wsd for n-best reranking and local language modeling in smt. In *Proceedings of the Sixth Workshop on Syntax, Semantics and Structure in Statistical Translation*, pages 1–9, Jeju, Republic of Korea. Association for Computational Linguistics.

Carpuat, M. and Wu, D. (2005). Word sense disambiguation vs. statistical machine translation. In *Proceedings of the 43rd Annual Meeting on Association for Computational Linguistics*, ACL '05, pages 387–394, Stroudsburg, PA, USA. Association for Computational Linguistics.

Declerck, T., Krieger, H.-U., Thomas, S. M., Buitelaar, P., O'Riain, S., Wunner, T., Maguet, G., McCrae, J., Spohr, D., and Montiel-Ponsoda, E. (2010). Ontology-based multilingual access to financial reports for sharing business knowledge across europe. In *Internal Financial Control Assessment Applying Multilingual Ontology Framework*.

Denkowski, M. and Lavie, A. (2011). Meteor 1.3: Automatic Metric for Reliable Optimization and Evaluation of Machine Translation Systems. In *Proceedings of the Sixth Workshop on Statistical Machine Translation*, pages 85–91, Edinburgh, Scotland. Association for Computational Linguistics.

Doddington, G. (2002). Automatic evaluation of machine translation quality using n-gram co-occurrence statistics. In *Proceedings of the second international conference on Human Language Technology Research*, HLT '02, pages 138–145.

Gabrilovich, E. and Markovitch, S. (2007). Computing semantic relatedness using wikipedia-based explicit semantic analysis. In *Proceedings of The Twentieth International Joint Conference for Artificial Intelligence*, pages 1606–1611, Hyderabad, India.

Klein, D. and Manning, C. D. (2003). Accurate unlexicalized parsing. In *Proceeding of the 41st annual meeting of the association for computational linguistics*, pages 423–430.

Koehn, P. (2005). Europarl: A Parallel Corpus for Statistical Machine Translation. In *Conference Proceedings: the tenth Machine Translation Summit*, pages 79–86. AAMT.

Koehn, P., Hoang, H., Birch, A., Callison-Burch, C., Federico, M., Bertoldi, N., Cowan, B., Shen, W., Moran, C., Zens, R., Dyer, C., Bojar, O., Constantin, A., and Herbst, E. (2007). Moses: Open Source Toolkit for Statistical Machine Translation. In *Proceedings of the 45th Annual Meeting of the ACL*, ACL '07, pages 177–180.

Mauser, A., Hasan, S., and Ney, H. (2009). Extending statistical machine translation with discriminative and trigger-based lexicon models. In *Conference on Empirical Methods in Natural Language Processing*, pages 210–217, Singapore.

McCrae, J., Espinoza, M., Montiel-Ponsoda, E., Aguado-de Cea, G., and Cimiano, P. (2011). Combining statistical and semantic approaches to the translation of ontologies and taxonomies. In *Fifth workshop on Syntax, Structure and Semantics in Statistical Translation (SSST-5)*.

Och, F. J. and Ney, H. (2003). A systematic comparison of various statistical alignment models. *Computational Linguistics*, 29.

Papineni, K., Roukos, S., Ward, T., and Zhu, W.-J. (2002). BLEU: A Method for Automatic Evaluation of Machine Translation. In *Proceedings of the 40th Annual Meeting of the Association for Computational Linguistics*, ACL '02, pages 311–318, Stroudsburg, PA, USA. Association for Computational Linguistics.

Patry, A. and Langlais, P. (2011). Going beyond word cooccurrences in global lexical selection for statistical machine translation using a multilayer perceptron. In *5th International Joint Conference on Natural Language Processing (IJCNLP'11)*, pages 658–666, Chiang Mai, Thailand.

Schmid, H. (1995). Improvements in part-of-speech tagging with an application to german. In *In Proceedings of the ACL SIGDAT-Workshop*, pages 47–50.

Snover, M., Dorr, B., Schwartz, R., Micciulla, L., and Makhoul, J. (2006). A study of translation edit rate with targeted human annotation. In *In Proceedings of Association for Machine Translation in the Americas*, pages 223–231.

Stolcke, A. (2002). Srilm-an extensible language modeling toolkit. In *Proceedings International Conference on Spoken Language Processing*, pages 257–286.

Wu, H., Wang, H., and Zong, C. (2008). Domain adaptation for statistical machine translation with domain dictionary and monolingual corpora. In *Proceedings of the 22nd International Conference on Computational Linguistics - Volume 1*, COLING '08, pages 993–1000.

Reversing Morphological Tokenization in English-to-Arabic SMT

Mohammad Salameh[†] **Colin Cherry**[‡] **Grzegorz Kondrak**[†]

[†]Department of Computing Science
University of Alberta
Edmonton, AB, T6G 2E8, Canada
{msalameh,gkondrak}@ualberta.ca

[‡]National Research Council Canada
1200 Montreal Road
Ottawa, ON, K1A 0R6, Canada
Colin.Cherry@nrc-cnrc.gc.ca

Abstract

Morphological tokenization has been used in machine translation for morphologically complex languages to reduce lexical sparsity. Unfortunately, when translating into a morphologically complex language, recombining segmented tokens to generate original word forms is not a trivial task, due to morphological, phonological and orthographic adjustments that occur during tokenization. We review a number of detokenization schemes for Arabic, such as rule-based and table-based approaches and show their limitations. We then propose a novel detokenization scheme that uses a character-level discriminative string transducer to predict the original form of a segmented word. In a comparison to a state-of-the-art approach, we demonstrate slightly better detokenization error rates, without the need for any hand-crafted rules. We also demonstrate the effectiveness of our approach in an English-to-Arabic translation task.

1 Introduction

Statistical machine translation (SMT) relies on tokenization to split sentences into meaningful units for easy processing. For morphologically complex languages, such as Arabic or Turkish, this may involve splitting words into morphemes. Throughout this paper, we adopt the definition of tokenization proposed by Habash (2010), which incorporates both morphological segmentation as well as orthographic character transformations. To use an English example, the word *tries* would be morphologically tokenized as *"try + s"*, which involves orthographic changes at morpheme boundaries to match the lexical form of each token. When translating into a tokenized language, the tokenization must be reversed to make the generated text readable and evaluable. Detokenization is the process of converting tokenized words into their original orthographically and morphologically correct surface form. This includes concatenating tokens into complete words and reversing any character transformations that may have taken place.

For languages like Arabic, tokenization can facilitate SMT by reducing lexical sparsity. Figure 1 shows how the morphological tokenization of the Arabic word وسيمنعهم "and he will prevent them" simplifies the correspondence between Arabic and English tokens, which in turn can improve the quality of word alignment, rule extraction and decoding. When translating from Arabic into English, the tokenization is a form of preprocessing, and the output translation is readable, space-separated English. However, when translating from English to Arabic, the output will be in a tokenized form, which cannot be compared to the original reference without detokenization. Simply concatenating the tokenized morphemes cannot fully reverse this process, because of character transformations that occurred during tokenization.

The techniques that have been proposed for the detokenization task fall into three categories (Badr et al., 2008). The simplest detokenization approach concatenates morphemes based on token markers without any adjustment. Table-based detokenization maps tokenized words into their surface form with a look-up table built by observing the tokenizer's in-

Proceedings of the NAACL HLT 2013 Student Research Workshop, pages 47–53,
Atlanta, Georgia, 13 June 2013.

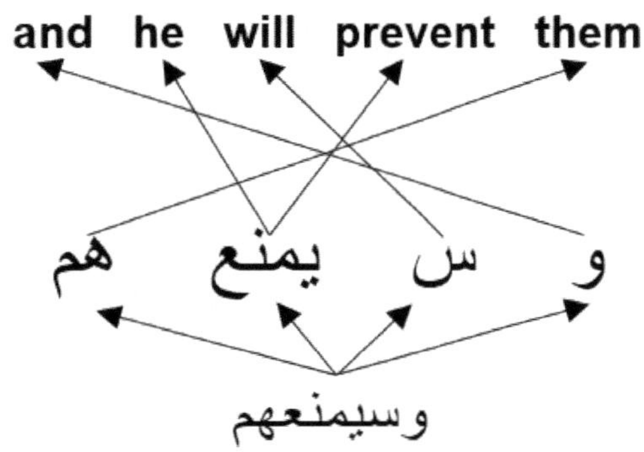

Figure 1: Alignment between tokenized form of *"wsymnςhm"* وسيمنعهم and its English translation.

put and output on large amounts of text. Rule-based detokenization relies on hand-built rules or regular expressions to convert the segmented form into the original surface form. Other techniques use combinations of these approaches. Each approach has its limitations: rule-based approaches are language specific and brittle, while table-based approaches fail to deal with sequences outside of their tables.

We present a new detokenization approach that applies a discriminative sequence model to predict the original form of the tokenized word. Like table-based approaches, our sequence model requires large amounts of tokenizer input-output pairs; but instead of building a table, we use these pairs as training data. By using features that consider large windows of within-word input context, we are able to intelligently transition between rule-like and table-like behavior.

Our experimental results on Arabic text demonstrate an improvement in terms of sentence error rate[1] of 11.9 points over a rule-based approach, and 1.1 points over a table-based approach that backs off to rules. More importantly, we achieve a slight improvement over the state-of-the-art approach of El Kholy and Habash (2012), which combines rules and tables, using a 5-gram language model to disambiguate conflicting table entries. In addition, our detokenization method results in a small BLEU improvement over a rule-based approach when applied to English-to-Arabic SMT.

2 Arabic Morphology

Compared to English, Arabic has rich and complex morphology. Arabic base words inflect to eight features. Verbs inflect for aspect, mood, person and voice. Nouns and adjectives inflect for case and state. Verbs, nouns and adjectives inflect for both gender and number. Furthermore, inflected base words can attract various optional clitics. Clitical prefixes include determiners, particle proclitics, conjunctions and question particles in strict order. Clitical suffixes include pronominal modifiers. As a result of clitic attachment, morpho-syntactic interactions sometimes cause changes in spelling or pronunciations.

Several tokenization schemes can be defined for Arabic, depending on the clitical level that the tokenization is applied to. In this paper, we use Penn Arabic Treebank (PATB) tokenization scheme, which El Kholy and Habash (2012) report as producing the best results for Arabic SMT. The PATB scheme detaches all clitics except for the definite article *Al* ال. Multiple prefix clitics are treated as one token.

Some Arabic letters present further ambiguity in text.[2] For example, the different forms of Hamzated Alif "أ إ" are usually written without the Hamza "ء". Likewise, when the letter Ya *'Y'* ي is present at the end of the word, it is sometimes written in the form of "Alif Maqsura" letter *'ý'* ى. Also, short vowels in Arabic are represented using diacritics, which are usually absent in written text. In order to deal with these ambiguities in SMT, normalization is often performed as a preprocessing step, which usually involves converting different forms of Alif and Ya to a single form. This decreases Arabic's lexical sparsity and improves SMT performance.

3 Related Work

Sadat and Habash (2006) address the issue of lexical sparsity by presenting different preprocessing schemes for Arabic-to-English SMT. The schemes include simple tokenization, orthographic normalization, and decliticization. The combination of these schemes results in improved translation out-

[1]Sentence error rate is the percentage of sentences containing at least one error after detokenization.

[2]We use Habash-Soudi-Buckwalter transliteration scheme (Habash, 2007) for all Arabic examples.

put. This is one of many studies on normalization and tokenization for translation from Arabic, which we will not attempt to review completely here.

Badr et al. (2008) show that tokenizing Arabic also has a positive influence on English-to-Arabic SMT. They apply two tokenization schemes on Arabic text, and introduce detokenization schemes through a rule-based approach, a table-based approach, and a combination of both. The combination approach detokenizes words first using the table, falling back on rules for sequences not found in the table.

El Kholy and Habash (2012) extend Badr's work by presenting a larger number of tokenization and detokenization schemes, and comparing their effects on SMT. They introduce an additional detokenization schemes based on the SRILM *disambig* utility (Stolcke, 2002), which utilizes a 5-gram untokenized language model to decide among different alternatives found in the table. They test their schemes on naturally occurring Arabic text and SMT output. Their newly introduced detokenization scheme outperforms the rule-based and table-based approaches introduced by Badr et al. (2008), establishing the current state-of-the-art.

3.1 Detokenization Schemes in Detail

Rule-based detokenization involves manually defining a set of transformation rules to convert a sequence of segmented tokens into their surface form. For example, the noun *"llrŷys"* للرئيس "to the president" is tokenized as *"l+ Alrŷys"* (*l+* "to" *Alrŷys* "the president") in the PATB tokenization scheme. Note that the definite article *"Al"* ال is kept attached to the noun. In this case, detokenization requires a character-level transformation after concatenation, which we can generalize using the rule:

$$l{+}Al \rightarrow ll.$$

Table 1 shows the rules provided by El Kholy and Habash (2012), which we employ throughout this paper.

There are two principal problems with the rule-based approach. First, rules fail to account for unusual cases. For example, the above rule mishandles cases where *"Al"* ال is a basic part of the stem and not the definite article *"the"*. Thus, 'l+ AlςAb' (*l+* "to" *AlςAb* "games") is erroneously detokenized to *llEAb* للعاب instead of the correct form is *"lAlςAb"* لالعاب. Second, rules may fail to handle sequences produced by tokenization errors. For example, the word *"bslTħ"* بسلطة "with power" can be erroneously tokenized as *"b+slT+h"*, while the correct tokenizations is *"b+slTħ"*. The erroneous tokenization will be incorrectly detokenized as *"bslTh"*.

Rule	Input	Output
l+Al+l? → ll	l+ Alrŷys	llrŷys
ħ+(*pron*) → t(*pron*)	Abnħ+hA	AbnthA
y+(*pron*) → A(*pron*)	Alqy+h	AlqAh
'+(*pron*) → ŷ	AntmA'+hm	AntmAŷhm
y+y → y	ςyny+y	ςyny
n+n → n	mn+nA	mnA
mn+m → mm	mn+mA	mmA
ςn+m → ςm	ςn+mA	ςmA
An+lA → AlA	An+lA	AlA

Table 1: Detokenization rules of El Kholy and Habash (2012), with examples. *pron* stands for pronominal clitic.

The table-based approach memorizes mappings between words and their tokenized form. Such a table is easily constructed by running the tokenizer on a large amount of Arabic text, and observing the input and output. The detokenization process consults this table to retrieve surface forms of tokenized words. In the case where a tokenized word has several observed surface forms, the most frequent form is selected. This approach fails when the sequence of tokenized words is not in the table. In morphologically complex languages like Arabic, an inflected base word can attrract many optional clitics, and tables may not include all different forms and inflections of a word.

The SRILM-disambig scheme introduced by El Kholy and Habash (2012) extends the table-based approach to use an untokenized Arabic language model to disambiguate among the different alternatives. Hence, this scheme can make context-dependent detokenization decisions, rather than always producing the most frequent surface form. Both the SRILM-disambig scheme and the table-based scheme have the option to fall back on either rules or simple concatenation for sequences missing from the table.

4 Detokenization as String Transduction

We propose to approach detokenization as a string transduction task. We train a discriminative transducer on a set of tokenized-detokenized word pairs. The set of pairs is initially aligned on the character level, and the alignment pairs become the operations that are applied during transduction. For detokenization, most operations simply copy over characters, but more complex rules such as *l+ Al* $\rightarrow$ *ll* are learned from the training data as well.

The tool that we use to perform the transduction is DIRECTL+, a discriminative, character-level string transducer, which was originally designed for letter-to-phoneme conversion (Jiampojamarn et al., 2008). To align the characters in each training example. DIRECTL+ uses an EM-based M2M-ALIGNER (Jiampojamarn et al., 2007). After alignment is complete, MIRA training repeatedly decodes the training set to tune the features that determine when each operation should be applied. The features include both n-gram source context and HMM-style target transitions. DIRECTL+ employs a fully discriminative decoder to learn character transformations and when they should be applied. The decoder resembles a monotone phrase-based SMT decoder, but is built to allow for hundreds of thousands of features.

The following example illustrates how string transduction applies to detokenization. The segmented and surface forms of *bbrAςthm* ببراعتهم "with their skill" constitute a training instance:

b+_brAςħ_+hm $\rightarrow$ *bbrAςthm*

The instance is aligned during the training phase as:

b+	_b	r	A	ς	ħ_	+	h	m
|	|	|	|	|	|	|	|	|
b	b	r	A	ς	t	ϵ	h	m

The underscore "_" indicates a space, while "ϵ" denotes an empty string. The following operations are extracted from the alignment:

b+ $\rightarrow$ b, _b $\rightarrow$ b, r $\rightarrow$ r, A $\rightarrow$ A, E $\rightarrow$ E, p_ $\rightarrow$ t, + $\rightarrow$ ϵ, h $\rightarrow$ h, m $\rightarrow$ m

During training, weights are assigned to features that associate operations with context. In our running example, the weight assigned to the b+ $\rightarrow$ b operation accounts for the operation itself, for the fact that the operation appears at the beginning of a word, and for the fact that it is followed by an underscore; in fact, we employ a context window of 5 characters to the left or right of the source substring "b+", creating a feature for each n-gram within that window.

Modeling the tokenization problem as string transduction has several advantages. The approach is completely language-independent. The context-sensitive rules are learned automatically from examples, without human intervention. The rules and features can be represented in a more compact way than the full mapping table required by table-based approaches, while still elegantly handling words that were not seen during training. Also, since the training data is generalized more efficiently than in simple memorization of complete tokenized-detokenized pairs, less training data should be needed to achieve good accuracy.

5 Experiments

This section presents two experiments that evaluate the effect of the detokenization schemes on both naturally occurring Arabic and SMT output.

5.1 Data

To build our data-driven detokenizers, we use the Arabic part of 4 Arabic-English parallel datasets from the Linguistic Data Consortium as training data. The data sets are: Arabic News (LDC2004T17), eTIRR (LDC2004E72), English translation of Arabic Treebank (LDC2005E46), and Ummah (LDC2004T18). The training data has 107K sentences. The Arabic part of the training data constitutes around 2.8 million words, 3.3 million tokens after tokenization, and 122K word types after filtering punctuation marks, Latin words and numbers (refer to Table 2 for detailed counts).

For training the SMT system's translation and reordering models, we use the same 4 datasets from LDC. We also use 200 Million words from LDC Arabic Gigaword corpus (LDC2011T11) to generate a 5-gram language model using SRILM toolkit (Stolcke, 2002).

We use NIST MT 2004 evaluation set for tuning (1075 sentences), and NIST MT 2005 evaluations set for testing (1056 sentences). Both MT04 and MT05 have multiple English references in order to evaluate Arabic-to-English translation. As we are translating into Arabic, we take the first English

Data set	Before	After
training set	122,720	61,943
MT04	8,201	2,542
MT05	7,719	2,429

Table 2: Type counts before and after tokenization.

translation to be our source in each case. We also use the Arabic halves of MT04 and MT05 as development and test sets for our experiments on naturally occurring Arabic. The tokenized Arabic is our input, with the original Arabic as our gold-standard detokenization.

The Arabic text of the training, development, testing set and language model are all tokenized using MADA 3.2 (Habash et al., 2009) with the Penn Arabic Treebank tokenization scheme. The English text in the parallel corpus is lower-cased and tokenized in the traditional sense to strip punctuation marks.

5.2 Experimental Setup

To train the detokenization systems, we generate a table of mappings from tokenized forms to surface forms based on the Arabic part of our 4 parallel datasets, giving us complete coverage of the output vocabulary of our SMT system. In the table-based approaches, if a tokenized form is mapped to more than one surface form, we use the most frequent surface form. For out-of-table words, we fall back on concatenation (in T) or rules (in T+R). For SRILM-Disambig detokenization, we maintain ambiguous table entries along with their frequencies, and we introduce a 5-gram language model to disambiguate detokenization choices in context. Like the table-based approaches, the Disambig approach can back off to either simple concatenation (T+LM) or rules (T+R+LM) for missing entries. The latter is a re-implementation of the state-of-the-art system presented by El Kholy and Habash (2012).

We train our discriminative string transducer using word types from the 4 LDC catalogs. We use M2M-ALIGNER to generate a 2-to-1 character alignments between tokenized forms and surface forms. For the decoder, we set Markov order to one, joint n-gram features to 5, n-gram size to 11, and context size to 5. This means the decoder can utilize contexts up to 11 characters long, allowing it to effectively memorize many words. We found these settings using grid search on the development set, NIST MT04.

Detokenization	WER	SER	BLEU
Baseline	1.710	34.3	26.30
Rules (R)	0.590	14.0	28.32
Table (T)	0.192	4.9	28.54
Table + Rules (T+R)	0.122	3.2	28.55
Disambig (T+LM)	0.164	4.1	28.53
Disambig (T+R+LM)	0.094	2.4	28.54
DIRECTL+	0.087	2.1	28.55

Table 3: Word and sentence error rate of detokenization schemes on the Arabic reference text of NIST MT05. BLEU score refers to English-Arabic SMT output.

For the SMT experiment, we use GIZA++ for the alignment between English and tokenized Arabic, and perform the translation using Moses phrase-based SMT system (Hoang et al., 2007), with a maximum phrase length of 5. We apply each detokenization scheme on the SMT tokenized Arabic output test set, and evaluate using the BLEU score (Papineni et al., 2002).

5.3 Results

Table 3 shows the performance of several detokenization schemes. For evaluation, we use the sentence and word error rates on naturally occurring Arabic text, and BLEU score on tokenized Arabic output of the SMT system. The baseline scheme, which is a simple concatenation of morphemes, introduces errors in over a third of all sentences. The table-based approach outperforms the rule-based approach, indicating that there are frequent exceptions to the rules in Table 1 that require memorization. Their combination (T+R) fares better, leveraging the strengths of both approaches. The addition of SRILM-Disambig produces further improvements as it uses a language model context to disambiguate the correct detokenized word form. Our system outperforms SRILM-Disambig by a very slight margin, indicating that the two systems are roughly equal. This is interesting, as it is able to do so by using only features derived from the tokenized word itself; unlike SRILM-Disambig, it has no access to the surrounding words to inform its decisions. In addition, it is able to achieve this level of performance without any manually constructed rules.

Improvements in detokenization do contribute to the BLEU score of our SMT system, but only to a point. Table 3 shows three tiers of performance, with no detokenization being the worst, the rules being better, and the various data-driven approaches performing best. After WER dips below 0.2, further improvements seem to no longer affect SMT quality. Note that BLEU scores are much lower overall than one would expect for the translation in the reverse direction, because of the morphological complexity of Arabic, and the use of one (as opposed to four) references for evaluation.

5.4 Analysis

The sentence error rate of 2.1 represents only 21 errors that our approach makes. Among those 21, 11 errors are caused by changing *p* to *h* and vice versa. This is due to writing *p* and *h* interchangeably. For example, *"AjmAly+h"* was detokenized as *"AjmAlyħ"* اجمالية instead of "AjmAlyh" اجماليه. Another 4 errors are caused by the lack of diacritization, which affects the choice of the Hamza form. For example,*"bnAŵh"* بناؤه, *"bnAŷh"* بنائه and *"bnA'h"* بناءه ("its building") are 3 different forms of the same word where the choice of Hamza ء is dependent on its diacritical mark or the mark of the character that precedes it. Another 3 errors are attributed to the case of the nominal which it inflects for. The case is affected by the context of the noun which DIRECTL+ has no access to. For example, *"mfkry+hm"* ("thinkers/Dual-Accusative") was detokenized as *"mfkrAhm"* مفكراهم (Dual-Nominative) instead of "mfkryhm" مفكريهم. The last 3 errors are special cases of *"An +y"* which can be detokenized correctly as either *"Any"* اني or *"Anny"* انني.

The table-based detokenization scheme fails in 54 cases. Among these instances, 44 cases are not in the mapping table, hence resolving back to simple concatenation ended with an error. Our transduction approach succeeds in detokenizing 42 cases out of the 54. The majority of these cases involves changing *p* to *h* and vice versa, and changing *l+Al* to *ll*. The only 2 instances where the tokenized word is in the mapping table but DIRECTL+ incorrectly detokenizes it are due to hamza case and p to h case described above. There are 4 instances of the same word/case where both the table scheme and DIRECTL+ fails due to error of tokenization by MADA, where the proper name *qwh* قوه is erroneously tokenized as *qw+p*. This shows that DIRECTL+ handles the OOV words correctly.

The Disambig(T+R+LM) erroneously detokenizes 27 instances, where 21 out of them are correctly tokenized by DIRECTL+. Most of the errors are due to the Hamza and p to h reasons. It seems that even with a large size language model, the SRILM utility needs a large mapping table to perform well. Only 4 instances were erroneously detokenized by both Disambig and DIRECTL+ due to Hamza and the case of the nominal.

The analysis shows that using small size training data, DIRECTL+ can achieve slightly better accuracy than SRILM scheme. The limitations of using table and rules are handled with DIRECTL+ as it is able to memorize more rules.

6 Conclusion and Future Work

In this paper, we addressed the detokenization problem for Arabic using DIRECTL+, a discriminative training model for string transduction. Our system performs the best among the available systems. It manages to solve problems caused by limitations of table-based and rule-based systems. This allows us to match the performance of the SRILM-disambig approach without using a language model or handcrafted rules. In the future, we plan to test our approach on other languages that have morphological characteristics similar to Arabic.

References

Ibrahim Badr, Rabih Zbib, and James Glass. 2008. Segmentation for English-to-Arabic statistical machine translation. In *Proceedings of ACL*, pages 153–156.

Ahmed El Kholy and Nizar Habash. 2012. Orthographic and morphological processing for English-Arabic statistical machine translation. *Machine Translation*, 26(1-2):25–45, March.

Nizar Habash, Owen Rambow, and Ryan Roth. 2009. Mada+tokan: A toolkit for Arabic tokenization, diacritization, morphological disambiguation, POS tagging, stemming and lemmatization. In *Proceedings of the Second International Conference on Arabic Language Resources and Tools.*

Nizar Habash. 2007. Arabic morphological representations for machine translation. In *Arabic Computational Morphology: Knowledge-based and Empirical Methods.*

Nizar Habash. 2010. *Introduction to Arabic Natural Language Processing*. Synthesis Lectures on Human Language Technologies. Morgan & Claypool Publishers.

Hieu Hoang, Alexandra Birch, Chris Callison-burch, Richard Zens, Rwth Aachen, Alexandra Constantin, Marcello Federico, Nicola Bertoldi, Chris Dyer, Brooke Cowan, Wade Shen, Christine Moran, and Ondrej Bojar. 2007. Moses: Open source toolkit for statistical machine translation. In *Annual Meeting of the Association for Computational Linguistics (ACL), demonstration session*, pages 177–180.

Sittichai Jiampojamarn, Grzegorz Kondrak, and Tarek Sherif. 2007. Applying many-to-many alignments and HMMs to letter-to-phoneme conversion. In *Proceedings of NAACL-HLT*, pages 372–379.

Sittichai Jiampojamarn, Colin Cherry, and Grzegorz Kondrak. 2008. Joint processing and discriminative training for letter-to-phoneme conversion. In *Proceedings of ACL-08: HLT*, pages 905–913.

Kishore Papineni, Salim Roukos, Todd Ward, and Wei jing Zhu. 2002. Bleu: a method for automatic evaluation of machine translation. In *Proceedings of 40th Annual Meeting of the Association for Computational Linguistics*, pages 311–318.

Fatiha Sadat and Nizar Habash. 2006. Combination of Arabic preprocessing schemes for statistical machine translation. In *Proceedings of the 21st International Conference on Computational Linguistics and the 44th annual meeting of the Association for Computational Linguistics*, pages 1–8.

Andreas Stolcke. 2002. SRILM - an extensible language modeling toolkit. In *Intl. Conf. Spoken Language Processing*, pages 901–904.

Statistical Machine Translation in Low Resource Settings

Ann Irvine
Center for Language and Speech Processing
Johns Hopkins University

Abstract

My thesis will explore ways to improve the performance of statistical machine translation (SMT) in low resource conditions. Specifically, it aims to reduce the dependence of modern SMT systems on expensive parallel data. We define low resource settings as having only small amounts of parallel data available, which is the case for many language pairs. All current SMT models use parallel data during training for extracting translation rules and estimating translation probabilities. The theme of our approach is the *integration of information from alternate data sources, other than parallel corpora*, into the statistical model. In particular, we focus on making use of large *monolingual* and *comparable* corpora. By augmenting components of the SMT framework, we hope to extend its applicability beyond the small handful of language pairs with large amounts of available parallel text.

1 Introduction

Statistical machine translation (SMT) systems are heavily dependent on parallel data. SMT doesn't work well when fewer than several million lines of bitext are available (Kolachina et al., 2012). When the available bitext is small, statistical models perform poorly due to the sparse word and phrase counts that define their parameters. Figure 1 gives a learning curve that shows this effect. As the amount of bitext approaches zero, performance drops drastically. In this thesis, we seek to modify the SMT model to reduce its dependence on parallel data and, thus, enable it to apply to new language pairs.

Specifically, we plan to address the following challenges that arise when using SMT systems in low resource conditions:

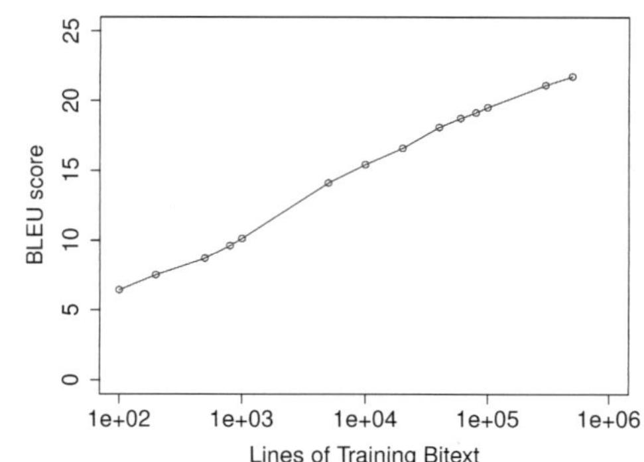

Figure 1: Learning curve that shows how SMT performance on the Spanish to English translation task increases with increasing amounts of parallel data. Performance is measured with BLEU and drops drastically as the amount of bitext approaches zero. These results use the Europarl corpus and the Moses phrase-based SMT framework, but the trend shown is typical.

- **Translating unknown words.** In the context of SMT, unknown words (or out-of-vocabulary, OOV) are defined as having never appeared in the source side of the training parallel corpus. When the training corpus is small, the percent of words which are unknown can be high.
- **Inducing phrase translations.** In high resource conditions, a word aligned bitext is used to extract a list of phrase pairs or translation rules which are used to translate new sentences. With more parallel data, this list is increasingly comprehensive. Using multi-word phrases instead of individual words as the basic translation unit has been shown to increase translation performance (Koehn et al., 2003). However, when the parallel corpus is small, so is the number of phrase pairs that can be extracted.
- **Estimating translation probabilities.** In the standard SMT pipeline, translation probabilities are estimated using relative frequency counts over the training bitext. However, when the bitext counts are sparse, probability esti-

Proceedings of the NAACL HLT 2013 Student Research Workshop, pages 54–61,
Atlanta, Georgia, 13 June 2013.

Language	#Words	Language	#Words
Nepali	0.4	Somali	0.5
Uzbek	1.4	Azeri	2.6
Tamil	3.7	Albanian	6.5
Bengali	6.6	Welsh	7.5
Bosnian	12.9	Latvian	40.2
Indonesian	21.8	Romanian	24.1
Serbian	25.8	Turkish	31.2
Ukrainian	37.6	Hindi	47.4
Bulgarian	49.5	Polish	104.5
Slovak	124.3	Urdu	287.2
Farsi	710.3	Spanish	972

Table 1: Millions of monolingual web crawl and Wikipedia word tokens

mates are likely to be noisy.

My thesis focuses on translating into English. We assume access to a small amount of parallel data, which is realistic, especially considering the recent success of crowdsourcing translations (Zaidan and Callison-Burch, 2011; Ambati, 2011; Post et al., 2012). Additionally, we assume access to larger monolingual corpora. Table 1 lists the 22 languages for which we plan to perform translation experiments, along with the total amount of monolingual data that we will use for each. We use web crawled time-stamped news articles and Wikipedia for each language. We have extracted the Wikipedia pages which are inter-lingually linked to English pages.

2 Translating Unknown Words

OOV words are a major challenge in low resource SMT settings. Here, we describe several approaches to identifying translations for unknown words.

2.1 Transliteration

For non-roman script languages, in some cases, OOV words may be *transliterated* rather than *translated.* This is often true for named entities, where transliterated words are pronounced approximately the same across languages but have different spellings in the source and target language alphabets (e.g. Russian Анна translates as English *Anna*). In the case of roman script languages, of course, such words are often translated correctly without change (e.g. French *Anna* translates as English *Anna*).

In my prior work, Irvine et al. (2010a) and Irvine et al. (2010b), I have presented a language-independent approach to gathering pairs of transliterated words (specifically, names) in a pair of languages, built a module to transliterate from one language to the other, and integrated the output into an end-to-end SMT system. In my thesis, I will use this technique to hypothesize translations for OOV words. Additionally, I plan to include techniques that build upon the one described in Hermjakob et al. (2008) in order to predict when words are likely to be transliterated rather than translated. That work uses features based on an Arabic named entity tagger. In our low resource setting, we cannot assume access to such off-the-shelf tools and must adapt this existing technique accordingly.

2.2 Bilingual Lexicon Induction

Bilingual lexicon induction is the task of identifying word translation pairs in source and target language monolingual or comparable corpora. The task is well-researched, however, in prior work, Irvine and Callison-Burch (2013), we were the first to propose using *supervised* methods. Because we assume access to some small amount of parallel data, we can extract a bilingual dictionary from it to use for positive supervision. In my prior work and in the thesis, we use the following signals estimated over comparable source and target language corpora: orthographic, topic, temporal, and contextual similarity. Here, we give brief descriptions of each.

Orthographic We measure orthographic similarity between a pair of words as the normalized[1] edit distance between the two words. For non-Roman script languages, we transliterate words into the Roman script before measuring orthographic similarity.

Topic We use monolingual Wikipedia pages to estimate topical signatures for each source and target language word. Signatures contain counts of how many times a given word appears on each interlingually linked Wikipedia page, and we use cosine similarity to compare pairs of signatures.

Temporal We use time-stamped web crawl data to estimate temporal signatures, which, for a given word, contain counts of how many times that word appeared in news articles with a certain date. We expect that source and target language words which are translations of one another will appear with similar frequencies over time in monolingual data.

[1]Normalized by the average of the lengths of the two words

Contextual We score monolingual contextual similarity by first collecting context vectors for each source and target language word. The context vector for a given word contain counts of how many times words appear in its context. We use bag of words contexts in a window of size two. We gather both source and target language contextual vectors from our web crawl data and Wikipedia data (separately).

Frequency Words that are translations of one another are likely to have similar relative frequencies in monolingual corpora. We measure the frequency similarity of two words as the absolute value of the difference between the log of their relative monolingual corpus frequencies.

We propose using a supervised approach to learning how to combine the above signals into a single discriminative binary classifier which predicts whether a source and target language word are translations of one another or not. Given a classification score for each source language word paired with all English candidates, we rerank candidates and evaluate on the top-k. We give some preliminary experimental details and results here.

We have access to bilingual dictionaries for the 22 languages listed in Table 1[2]. For each language, we choose up to $8,000$ source language words among those that occur in the monolingual data at least three times and that have at least one translation in our dictionary. We randomly divide the source language words into three equally sized sets for training, development, and testing. We use the training data to train a classifier, the development data to choose the best classification settings and feature set, and the test set for evaluation.

For all experiments, we use a linear classifier trained by stochastic gradient descent to minimize squared error[3] and perform 100 passes over the training data.[4] The binary classifiers predict whether a pair of words are translations of one another or not. The translations in our training data serve as positive supervision, and the source language words in

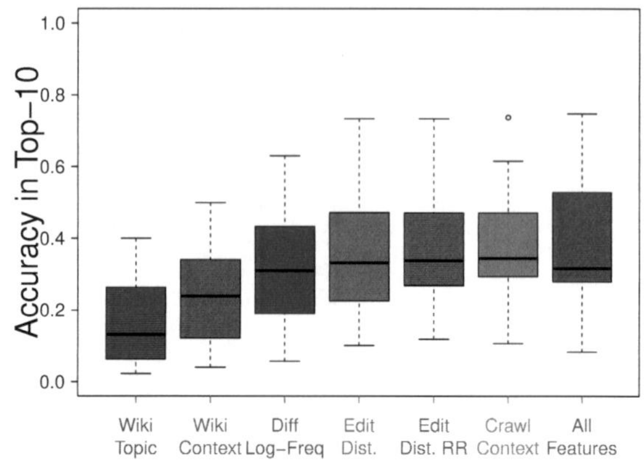

Figure 2: Performance goes up as features are greedily added to the feature space. Mean performance is slightly higher using this subset of six features (second to last bar) than using all features (last bar). Each plot represents results over our 22 languages.

the training data paired with random English words[5] serve as negative supervision. We used our development data to tune the number of negative examples to three for each positive example. At test time, after scoring all source language words in the test set paired with all English words in our candidate set,[6] we rank the English candidates by their classification scores and evaluate accuracy in the top-k.

We use raw similarity scores based on the signals enumerated above as features. Additionally, for each source word, we rank all English candidates with respect to each signal and include their reciprocal ranks as another set of features. Finally, we include a binary feature that indicates if a given source and target word are identical strings or not.

We train classifiers separately for each of the 22 languages listed in Table 1, and the learned weights vary based on, for example, corpora size and the relatedness of the source language and English (e.g. edit distance is informative if there are many cognates). When we use the trained classifier to predict which English words are translations of a given source word, all English words appearing at least five times in our monolingual data are candidates, and we rank them by their classification scores.

Figure 2, from left to right, shows a greedy search

[2]Details about the dictionaries in work under review.

[3]We tried using logistic rather than linear regression, but performance differences on our development set were very small and not statistically significant.

[4]We use `http://hunch.net/~vw/` version 6.1.4, and run it with the following arguments that affect how updates are made in learning: –exact adaptive norm –power t 0.5

[5]Among those that appear at least five times in our monolingual data, consistent with our candidate set.

[6]All English words appearing at least five times in our monolingual data. In practice, we further limit the set to those that occur in the top-1000 ranked list according to at least one of our signals.

Lang	MRR	Supv.	Lang	MRR	Supv.
Nepali	11.2	13.6	Somali	16.7	18.1
Uzbek	23.2	29.6	Azeri	16.1	29.4
Tamil	28.4	33.3	Albanian	32.0	45.3
Bengali	19.3	32.8	Welsh	36.1	56.4
Bosnian	32.6	52.8	Latvian	29.6	47.7
Indonesian	41.5	63.5	Romanian	53.3	71.6
Serbian	29.0	33.3	Turkish	31.4	52.1
Ukrainian	29.7	46.0	Hindi	18.2	34.6
Bulgarian	40.2	57.9	Polish	47.4	67.1
Slovak	34.6	53.5	Urdu	13.2	21.2
Farsi	10.5	21.1	Spanish	74.8	85.0

Table 2: Top-10 Accuracy on test set. Performance increases for all languages moving from the baseline (*MRR*) to discriminative training (*Supv*).

for the best subset of features. The Wikipedia topic score is the most informative stand-alone feature, and Wikipedia context is the most informative second feature. Adding features to the model beyond the six shown in the figure does not yield additional performance gains over our set of languages.

We use a model based on the six features shown in Figure 2 to score and rank English translation candidates for the test set words in each language.

Our unsupervised baseline method is based on ranked lists derived from each of the signals listed above. For each source word, we generate ranked lists of English candidates using the following six signals: Crawls Context, Crawls Time, Wikipedia Context, Wikipedia Topic, Edit distance, and Log Frequency Difference. Then, for each English candidate we compute its mean reciprocal rank[7] (MRR) based on the six ranked lists. The baseline ranks English candidates according to the MRR scores. For evaluation, we use the same test sets, accuracy metric, and correct translations.

Table 2 gives results for the baseline and our supervised technique. Across languages, the average top-10 accuracy using the baseline is 30.4, and using our technique it is 43.9, about *44% higher*.

In Section 3 we use the same features to score all *phrase pairs* in a phrase-based MT model and include them as features in tuning and decoding.

[7]The MRR of the jth English word, e_j, is $\frac{1}{N}\sum_{i=1}^{N}\frac{1}{rank_{ij}}$, where N is the number of signals and $rank_{ij}$ is e_j's rank according to signal i.

2.3 Distributed Representations

Our third method for inducing OOV translations employs a similar intuition to that of contextual similarity. However, unlike standard contextual vectors that represent words as large vectors of counts of nearby words, we propose to use *distributed representations*. These word representations are low-dimensional and are induced iteratively using the distributed representations of nearby words, not the nearby words themselves. Using distributed representations helps to alleviate data sparsity problems.

Recently, Klementiev et al. (2012b) induced distributed representations for the crosslingual setting. There, the induced embedding is learned jointly over multiple languages so that the representations of semantically similar words end up "close" to one another irrespective of language. They simultaneously use large monolingual corpora to induce representations for words in each language and use parallel data to bring the representations together across languages. The intuition for their approach to crosslingual representation induction comes from the multitask learning setup of Cavallanti et al. (2010). They apply this set-up to a variant of a neural probabilistic language model (Bengio et al., 2003).

In my thesis, I propose to use the distributed representations proposed by Klementiev et al. (2012b) in order to induce translations for OOV words. Additionally, I plan to learn how to compose the representations of individual words in a phrase into a single representation, allowing for the induction of *phrase* translations in addition to single words.

3 Inducing and Scoring a Phrase Table

Although by extracting OOV *word* translations we may increase the coverage of our SMT model, inducing *phrase* translations may increase performance further. In order to do so, we need to be able to score pairs of phrases to determine which have high translation probabilities. Furthermore, using alternate sources of data to score phrase pairs directly extracted from a small bitext may help distinguish good translation pairs from bad ones, which could result from incorrect word alignments, for example. In moving from words to phrases, we make use of many of the same techniques described in Section 2. Here, I present several proposals for addressing the major additional challenges that arise for phrases, and Section 4 presents some experimental results.

3.1 Phrase translation induction

The difficulty in inducing a comprehensive set of phrase translations is that the number of phrases, on both the source and target side, is very large. In moving from the induction of word translations to phrase translations, the number of comparisons necessary to do an exhaustive search becomes infeasible. I propose to explore several ways to speed up that search in my thesis:

- Use distributed phrase representations.
- Use filters to limit the phrase pair search space. Filters should be fast and could include information such as word translations, phrase lengths, and monolingual frequencies.
- Predict when phrases should be translated as a unit, rather than compositionally. If it is possible to accurately translate a phrase compositionally from its word translations, then there is no need to induce a translation for the phrase.

3.2 Phrase translation scoring

In our prior work, Klementiev et al. (2012a), we have started to explore scoring a phrase table using comparable corpora. Given a set of phrase pairs, either induced or extracted from a small bitext, the idea is to score them using the same signals derived from comparable corpora described in the context of bilingual lexicon induction in Section 2.2. No matter the source of the phrase pairs, the hope is that such scores will help an SMT model distinguish between good and bad translations. We estimate both *phrasal* and *lexical* similarity features over phrase pairs. We estimate the first using contextual, temporal, and topical signatures over entire phrases. We estimate the latter by using the *lexical* contextual, temporal, topical, and orthographic signatures of *each word in each phrase*. We use phrasal word alignments in order to compute the *lexical* similarity between phrases. That is, we compute each similarity metric for each pair of aligned words and then, for each similarity metric, average over the word pairs. This approach is analogous to the lexical weighting feature introduced by Koehn et al. (2003).

Language	Train Words	Dev OOV Word Types	Dev OOV Word Tokens
Tamil	452k	44%	25%
Bengali	272k	37%	18%
Hindi	708k	34%	11%

Table 3: Information about datasets released by Post et al. (2012). Training data gives the number of words in the source language training set. OOV rates give the percent of development set word types and work tokens that do not appear in the training data.

4 Preliminary Results

Here we show preliminary results using our methods for translating OOV words and our methods for scoring a phrase table in end-to-end low resource machine translation. Post et al. (2012) used Amazon's Mechanical Turk to collect a small parallel corpus for several Indian languages. In our experiments, we use their Tamil, Bengali, and Hindi datasets. We use the data splits given by Post et al. (2012) and, following that work, report results on the devtest set. Table 3 shows statistics about the datasets.

In our experiments, we use the Moses phrase-based machine translation framework (Koehn et al., 2007). For each language, we extract a phrase table from the training data with a phrase limit of seven and, like Post et al. (2012), use the English side of the training data to train a language model. Throughout our experiments, we use MIRA (Chiang et al., 2009) for tuning the feature set.

Our experiments compare the following:

- A baseline phrase-based model, using phrase pairs extracted from the training data and the standard phrasal and lexical translation probabilities based on the bitext.
- Baseline supplemented with word translations induced by our baseline unsupervised bilingual lexicon induction method (Section 2.2)
- Baseline supplemented with word translations induced by our supervised bilingual lexicon induction methods (Section 2.2).
- Baseline model supplemented with additional features, estimated over comparable corpora (Section 3.2).
- Baseline model supplemented with induced word translations and also additional features.

Table 4 shows our results. Adding additional phrase table features increased BLEU scores from

Experiment	K	Tamil BLEU	Tamil Diff.	Bengali BLEU	Bengali Diff.	Hindi BLEU	Hindi Diff.
Baseline		9.16		12.14		14.85	
+ Mono. Features		9.70	+0.54	12.54	+0.40	15.16	+0.31
+ Unsupervised Word Translations	1	9.33	+0.17	12.11	-0.03	15.37	+0.52
+ Supervised Word Translations	1	9.76	+0.60	12.38	+0.24	15.64	+0.79
+ Mono. Feats. & Sup. Trans.	1	10.20	+1.04	**13.01**	**+0.87**	15.84	+0.99
+ Mono. Feats. & Sup. Trans.	5	**10.41**	**+1.25**	12.64	+0.50	**16.02**	**+1.17**
+ Mono. Feats. & Sup. Trans.	10	10.12	+0.96	12.57	+0.43	15.86	+1.01

Table 4: BLEU performance gains that target coverage and accuracy separately and together. We add the top-K ranked translations for each OOV source word.

0.31 BLEU points for Hindi to 0.54 for Tamil.

Next, we monolingually induced translations for all development and test set source words. We experimented with adding translations for source words with low training data frequencies in addition to OOV words but did not observe BLEU improvements beyond what was gained by translating OOVs alone. Our BLEU score gains that result from improving OOV coverage, *+Supervised Word Translations*, range from 0.24 for Bengali to 0.79 for Hindi and outperform the unsupervised lexicon induction baseline for all three languages.

Using comparable corpora to supplement both the feature space and the coverage of OOVs results in translations that are better than applying either technique alone. For all languages, the BLEU improvements are approximately additive. For Tamil, the total BLEU point gain is 1.25, and it is 1.17 for Hindi and 0.87 for Bengali. Table 4 shows results as we add the top-k ranked translation for each OOV word and vary k. For Tamil and Hindi, we get a slight boost by adding the top-5 translations instead of the single best but get no further gains with the top-10.

5 Previous Work

Prior work on bilingual lexicon induction has shown that a variety of signals derived from monolingual data, including distributional, temporal, topic, and string similarity, are informative (Rapp, 1995; Fung and Yee, 1998; Koehn and Knight, 2002; Schafer and Yarowsky, 2002; Monz and Dorr, 2005; Huang et al., 2005; Schafer, 2006; Klementiev and Roth, 2006; Haghighi et al., 2008; Mimno et al., 2009; Mausam et al., 2010; Daumé and Jagarlamudi, 2011). This thesis builds upon this work and uses a diverse set of signals for translating full sentences, not just words. Recently, Ravi and Knight (2011), Dou and Knight (2012), and Nuhn et al. (2012) have worked toward learning a phrase-based translation model from monolingual corpora, relying on *decipherment* techniques. In contrast to that research thread, we make the realistic assumption that a small parallel corpus is available for our low resource languages. With a small parallel corpus, we are able to take advantage of supervised techniques, changing the problem setting dramatically.

Since the early 2000s, the AVENUE (Carbonell et al., 2002; Probst et al., 2002; Lavie et al., 2003) project has researched ways to rapidly develop MT systems for low-resource languages. In contrast to that work, my thesis will focus on a language-independent approach as well as integrating techniques into current state-of-the-art SMT frameworks. In her thesis, Gangadharaiah (2011) tackles several data sparsity issues within the example-based machine translation (EBMT) framework. Her work attempts to tackle some of the same data sparsity issues that we do including, in particular, phrase table coverage. However, our models for doing so are quite different and focus much more on the use of a variety of new non-parallel data resources.

Other approaches to low resource machine translation include extracting parallel sentences from comparable corpora (e.g. Smith et al. (2010)) and translation crowdsourcing. Our efforts are orthogonal and complementary to these.

6 Conclusion

My thesis will explore using alternative data sources, other than parallel text, to inform statistical machine translation models. In particular, I will build upon a long thread of research on bilingual lexicon induction from comparable corpora. The result of my thesis will be broadening the applicability of current SMT frameworks to language pairs and domains for which parallel data is limited.

7 Acknowledgements

The research presented in this paper was done in collaboration with my advisor, Chris Callison-Burch. This material is based on research sponsored by DARPA under contract HR0011-09-1-0044 and by the Johns Hopkins University Human Language Technology Center of Excellence. The views and conclusions contained in this publication are those of the authors and should not be interpreted as representing official policies or endorsements of DARPA or the U.S. Government.

References

Vamshi Ambati. 2011. *Active Learning for Machine Translation in Scarce Data Scenarios*. Ph.D. thesis, Carnegie Mellon University.

Yoshua Bengio, Réjean Ducharme, Pascal Vincent, and Christian Janvin. 2003. A neural probabilistic language model. *Journal of Machine Learning Research (JMLR)*, 3:1137–1155.

Jaime G. Carbonell, Katharina Probst, Erik Peterson, Christian Monson, Alon Lavie, Ralf D. Brown, and Lori S. Levin. 2002. Automatic rule learning for resource-limited mt. In *Proceedings of the Conference of the Association for Machine Translation in the Americas (AMTA)*.

Giovanni Cavallanti, Nicoló Cesa-bianchi, and Claudio Gentile. 2010. Linear algorithms for online multitask classification. *Journal of Machine Learning Research (JMLR)*, 11:2901–2934.

David Chiang, Kevin Knight, and Wei Wang. 2009. 11,001 new features for statistical machine translation. In *Proceedings of the Conference of the North American Chapter of the Association for Computational Linguistics (NAACL)*.

Hal Daumé, III and Jagadeesh Jagarlamudi. 2011. Domain adaptation for machine translation by mining unseen words. In *Proceedings of the Conference of the Association for Computational Linguistics (ACL)*.

Qing Dou and Kevin Knight. 2012. Large scale decipherment for out-of-domain machine translation. In *Proceedings of the Joint Conference on Empirical Methods in Natural Language Processing and Computational Natural Language Learning*.

Pascale Fung and Lo Yuen Yee. 1998. An IR approach for translating new words from nonparallel, comparable texts. In *Proceedings of the Conference of the Association for Computational Linguistics (ACL)*.

Rashmi Gangadharaiah. 2011. *Coping with Data-sparsity in Example-based Machine Translation*. Ph.D. thesis, Carnegie Mellon University.

Aria Haghighi, Percy Liang, Taylor Berg-Kirkpatrick, and Dan Klein. 2008. Learning bilingual lexicons from monolingual corpora. In *Proceedings of the Conference of the Association for Computational Linguistics (ACL)*.

Ulf Hermjakob, Kevin Knight, and Hal DaumŐ Iii. 2008. Name translation in statistical machine translation learning when to transliterate. In *Proceedings of the Conference of the Association for Computational Linguistics (ACL)*.

Fei Huang, Ying Zhang, and Stephan Vogel. 2005. Mining key phrase translations from web corpora. In *Proceedings of the Conference on Empirical Methods in Natural Language Processing (EMNLP)*.

Ann Irvine and Chris Callison-Burch. 2013. Supervised bilingual lexicon induction with multiple monolingual signals. In *Proceedings of the Conference of the North American Chapter of the Association for Computational Linguistics (NAACL)*.

Ann Irvine, Chris Callison-Burch, and Alexandre Klementiev. 2010a. Transliterating from all languages. In *Proceedings of the Conference of the Association for Machine Translation in the Americas (AMTA)*.

Ann Irvine, Mike Kayser, Zhifei Li, Wren Thornton, and Chris Callison-Burch. 2010b. Integrating output from specialized modules in machine translation: transliterations in joshua. *Prague Bulletin of Mathematical Linguistics*, pages 107–116.

Alexandre Klementiev and Dan Roth. 2006. Weakly supervised named entity transliteration and discovery from multilingual comparable corpora. In *Proceedings of the Conference of the Association for Computational Linguistics (ACL)*.

Alex Klementiev, Ann Irvine, Chris Callison-Burch, and David Yarowsky. 2012a. Toward statistical machine translation without parallel corpora. In *Proceedings of the Conference of the European Association for Computational Linguistics (EACL)*.

Alexandre Klementiev, Ivan Titov, and Binod Bhattarai. 2012b. Inducing crosslingual distributed representations of words. In *Proceedings of the International Conference on Computational Linguistics (COLING)*.

Philipp Koehn and Kevin Knight. 2002. Learning a translation lexicon from monolingual corpora. In *ACL Workshop on Unsupervised Lexical Acquisition*.

Philipp Koehn, Franz Joseph Och, and Daniel Marcu. 2003. Statistical phrase-based translation. In *Proceedings of the Conference of the North American Chapter of the Association for Computational Linguistics (NAACL)*.

Philipp Koehn, Hieu Hoang, Alexandra Birch, Chris Callison-Burch, Marcello Federico, Nicola Bertoldi, Brooke Cowan, Wade Shen, Christine Moran, Richard

Zens, Chris Dyer, Ondrej Bojar, Alexandra Constantin, and Evan Herbst. 2007. Moses: Open source toolkit for statistical machine translation. In *Proceedings of the Conference of the Association for Computational Linguistics (ACL)*.

Prasanth Kolachina, Nicola Cancedda, Marc Dymetman, and Sriram Venkatapathy. 2012. Prediction of learning curves in machine translation. In *Proceedings of the Conference of the Association for Computational Linguistics (ACL)*.

Alon Lavie, Stephan Vogel, Lori Levin, Erik Peterson, Katharina Probst, Ariadna Font, Rachel Reynolds, Jaime Carbonelle, and Richard Cohen. 2003. Experiments with a Hindi-to-English transfer-based MT system under a miserly data scenario. *ACM Transactions on Asian Language Information Processing (TALIP)*, 2.

Mausam, Stephen Soderland, Oren Etzioni, Daniel S. Weld, Kobi Reiter, Michael Skinner, Marcus Sammer, and Jeff Bilmes. 2010. Panlingual lexical translation via probabilistic inference. *Artificial Intelligence*, 174:619–637, June.

David Mimno, Hanna Wallach, Jason Naradowsky, David Smith, and Andrew McCallum. 2009. Polylingual topic models. In *Proceedings of the Conference on Empirical Methods in Natural Language Processing (EMNLP)*.

Christof Monz and Bonnie J. Dorr. 2005. Iterative translation disambiguation for cross-language information retrieval. In *Proceedings of the Conference on Research and Developments in Information Retrieval (SIGIR)*.

Malte Nuhn, Arne Mauser, and Hermann Ney. 2012. Deciphering foreign language by combining language models and context vectors. In *Proceedings of the Conference of the Association for Computational Linguistics (ACL)*.

Matt Post, Chris Callison-Burch, and Miles Osborne. 2012. Constructing parallel corpora for six indian languages via crowdsourcing. In *Proceedings of the Workshop on Statistical Machine Translation (WMT)*.

Katharina Probst, Lori Levin, Erik Peterson, Alon Lavie, and Jaime Carbonell. 2002. MT for minority languages using elicitation-based learning of syntactic transfer rules. *Machine Translation*, 17:245–270, December.

Reinhard Rapp. 1995. Identifying word translations in non-parallel texts. In *Proceedings of the Conference of the Association for Computational Linguistics (ACL)*.

Reinhard Rapp. 1999. Automatic identification of word translations from unrelated English and German corpora. In *Proceedings of the Conference of the Association for Computational Linguistics (ACL)*.

Sujith Ravi and Kevin Knight. 2011. Deciphering foreign language. In *Proceedings of the Conference of the Association for Computational Linguistics (ACL)*.

Charles Schafer and David Yarowsky. 2002. Inducing translation lexicons via diverse similarity measures and bridge languages. In *Proceedings of the Conference on Natural Language Learning (CoNLL)*.

Charles Schafer. 2006. *Translation Discovery Using Diverse Similarity Measures*. Ph.D. thesis, Johns Hopkins University.

Jason R. Smith, Chris Quirk, and Kristina Toutanova. 2010. Extracting parallel sentences from comparable corpora using document level alignment. In *Proceedings of the Conference of the North American Chapter of the Association for Computational Linguistics (NAACL)*.

Omar F. Zaidan and Chris Callison-Burch. 2011. Crowdsourcing translation: Professional quality from non-professionals. In *Proceedings of the Conference of the Association for Computational Linguistics (ACL)*.

Large-Scale Paraphrasing for Natural Language Understanding

Juri Ganitkevitch
Center for Language and Speech Processing
Johns Hopkins University
juri@cs.jhu.edu

Abstract

We examine the application of data-driven paraphrasing to natural language understanding. We leverage bilingual parallel corpora to extract a large collection of syntactic paraphrase pairs, and introduce an adaptation scheme that allows us to tackle a variety of text transformation tasks via paraphrasing. We evaluate our system on the sentence compression task. Further, we use distributional similarity measures based on context vectors derived from large monolingual corpora to annotate our paraphrases with an orthogonal source of information. This yields significant improvements in our compression system's output quality, achieving state-of-the-art performance. Finally, we propose a refinement of our paraphrases by classifying them into natural logic entailment relations. By extending the synchronous parsing paradigm towards these entailment relations, we will enable our system to perform recognition of textual entailment.

1 Introduction

In this work, we propose an extension of current paraphrasing methods to tackle natural language understanding problems. We create a large set of paraphrase pairs in a data-driven fashion, rank them based on a variety of similarity metrics, and attach an entailment relation to each pair, facilitating natural logic inference. The resulting resource has potential applications to a variety of NLP applications, including summarization, query expansion, question answering, and recognizing textual entailment.

Specifically, we build on Callison-Burch (2007)'s pivot-based paraphrase extraction method, which uses bilingual parallel data to learn English *phrase pairs* that share the same meaning. Our approach extends the pivot method to learn meaning-preserving *syntactic transformations* in English. We represent these using synchronous context-free grammars (SCFGs). This representation allows us to re-use a lot of machine translation machinery to perform monolingual text-to-text generation. We demonstrate the method on a sentence compression task (Ganitkevitch et al., 2011).

To improve the system, we then incorporate features based on monolingual distributional similarity. This orthogonal source of signal allows us to re-scores the bilingually-extracted paraphrases using information drawn from large monolingual corpora. We show that the monolingual distributional scores yield significant improvements over a baseline that scores paraphrases only with bilingually-extracted features (Ganitkevitch et al., 2012).

Further, we propose a semantics for paraphrasing by classifying each paraphrase pair with one of the entailment relation types defined by natural logic (MacCartney, 2009). Natural logic is used to perform inference over pairs of natural language phrases, like our paraphrase pairs. It defines a set of relations including, equivalence ($\equiv$), forward- and backward-entailments ($\sqsubset$, $\sqsupset$), antonyms ($\wedge$), and others. We will build a classifier for our paraphrases that uses features extracted from annotated resources like WordNet and distributional information gathered over large text corpora to assign one or more entailment relations to each paraphrase pair. We will evaluate the entailment assignments by applying this enhanced paraphrasing system to the task of recognizing textual entailment (RTE).

2 Extraction of Syntactic Paraphrases from Bitexts

A variety of different types of corpora have been used to automatically induce paraphrase collections for English (see Madnani and Dorr (2010) for a sur-

Proceedings of the NAACL HLT 2013 Student Research Workshop, pages 62–68,
Atlanta, Georgia, 13 June 2013.

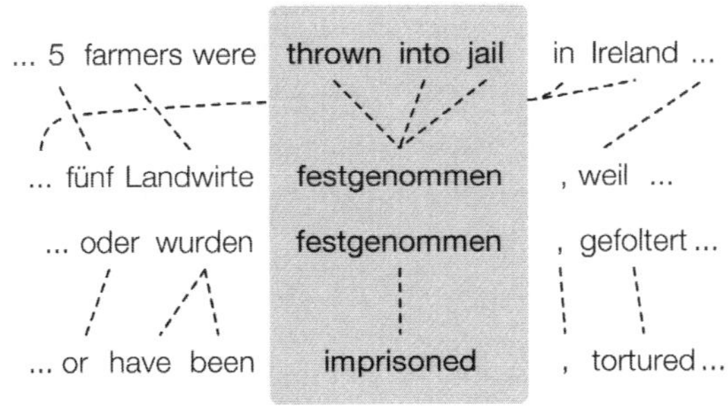

Figure 1: An example of pivot-based phrasal paraphrase extraction – we assume English phrases that translate to a common German phrase to be paraphrases. Thus we extract "imprisoned" as a paraphrase of "thrown into jail."

Possessive rule		
$NP \rightarrow$	the NN of the NNP	the NNP's NN
$NP \rightarrow$	the NP made by NN	the NN's NP
Dative shift		
$VP \rightarrow$	give NN to NP	give NP the NN
$VP \rightarrow$	provide NP_1 to NP_2	give NP_2 NP_1
Partitive constructions		
$NP \rightarrow$	CD of the NN	CD NN
$NP \rightarrow$	all NN	all of the NN
Reduced relative clause		
$SBAR/S \rightarrow$	although PRP VBP that	although PRP VBP
$ADJP \rightarrow$	very JJ that S	JJ S

Table 1: A selection of example paraphrase patterns extracted by our system. These rules demonstrate that, using the pivot approach from Figure 1, our system is capable of learning meaning-preserving syntactic transformations in English.

vey of these methods). Bannard and Callison-Burch (2005) extracted phrasal paraphrases from bitext by using foreign language phrases as a *pivot*: if two English phrases e_1 and e_2 both translate to a foreign phrase f, they assume that e_1 and e_2 are paraphrases of one another. Figure 1 gives an example of a phrasal paraphrase extracted by Bannard and Callison-Burch (2005).

Since "thrown into jail" is aligned to multiple German phrases, and since each of those German phrases align back to a variety of English phrases, the method extracts a wide range of possible paraphrases including good paraphrase like: *imprisoned* and *thrown into prison*. It also produces less good paraphrases like: *in jail* and *put in prison for*, and bad paraphrases, such as *maltreated* and *protection*, because of noisy/inaccurate word alignments and other problems. To rank these, Bannard and Callison-Burch (2005) derive a paraphrase probability $p(e_1|e_2)$:

$$p(e_2|e_1) \approx \sum_f p(e_2|f)p(f|e_1), \tag{1}$$

where the $p(e_i|f)$ and $p(f|e_i)$ are translation probabilities estimated from the bitext (Brown et al., 1990; Koehn et al., 2003).

We extend this method to extract *syntactic paraphrases* (Ganitkevitch et al., 2011). Table 1 shows example paraphrases produced by our system. While phrasal systems memorize phrase pairs without any further generalization, a syntactic paraphrasing system can learn more generic patterns. These can be better applied to unseen data. The paraphrases implementing the *possessive rule* and the *dative shift* shown in Table 1 are good examples of this: the two noun-phrase arguments to the expressions are abstracted to nonterminals while each rule's lexicalization provides an appropriate frame of evidence for the transform.

2.1 Formal Representation

In this proposal we focus on a paraphrase model based on *synchronous context-free grammar* (SCFG). The SCFG formalism (Aho and Ullman, 1972) was repopularized for statistical machine translation by (Chiang, 2005). An *probabilistic* SCFG $\mathcal{G}$ contains rules $\mathbf{r}$ of the form $\mathbf{r} = C \rightarrow \langle \gamma, \alpha, \sim, w \rangle$. A rule $\mathbf{r}$'s left-hand side C is a nonterminal, while its right-hands sides γ and α can be mixed strings of words and nonterminal symbols. There is a one-to-one correspondency between the nonterminals in γ and α. Each rule is assigned a cost $w_\mathbf{r} \geq 0$, reflecting its likelihood.

To compute the cost $w_\mathbf{r}$ of the application of a rule $\mathbf{r}$, we define a set of feature functions $\vec{\varphi} = \{\varphi_1 ... \varphi_N\}$ that are combined in a log-linear model. The model weights are set to maximize a task-dependent objective function.

2.2 Syntactic Paraphrase Rules via Bilingual Pivoting

Our paraphrase acquisition method is based on the extraction of syntactic translation rules in statistical machine translation (SMT). In SMT, SCFG rules are extracted from English-foreign sentence pairs that are automatically parsed and word-aligned. For a

	CR	Meaning	Grammar
Reference	0.80	4.80	4.54
ILP	0.74	3.44	**3.41**
PP	0.78	3.53	2.98
PP + n-gram	0.80	3.65	3.16
PP + syntax	0.79	**3.70**	3.26
Random Deletions	0.78	2.91	2.53

Table 2: Results of the human evaluation on longer compressions: pairwise compression ratios (CR), meaning and grammaticality scores. Bold indicates a statistically significant best result at $p < 0.05$. The scores range from 1 to 5, 5 being perfect.

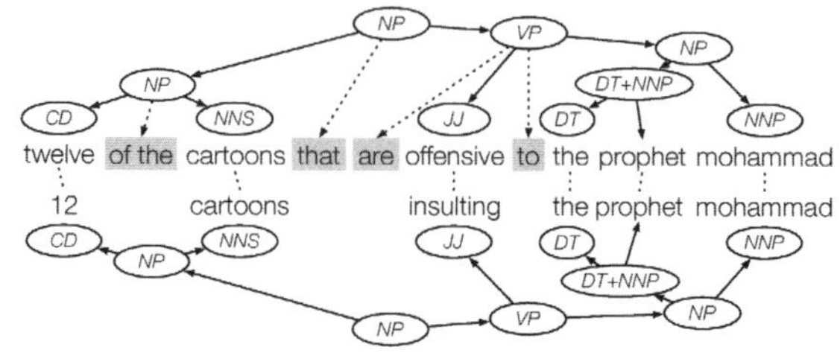

Figure 2: An example of a synchronous paraphrastic derivation in sentence compression.

foreign phrase the corresponding English phrase is found via the word alignments. This phrase pair is turned into an SCFG rule by assigning a left-hand side nonterminal symbol, corresponding to the syntactic constituent that dominates the English phrase. To introduce nonterminals into the right-hand sides of the rule, we can replace corresponding sub-phrases in the English and foreign phrases with nonterminal symbols. Doing this for all sentence pairs in a bilingual parallel corpus results in a *translation grammar* that serves as the basis for syntactic machine translation.

To create a *paraphrase grammar* from a translation grammar, we extend the syntactically informed pivot approach of (Callison-Burch, 2008) to the SCFG model: for each pair of translation rules $\mathbf{r}_1$ and $\mathbf{r}_2$ with matching left-hand side nonterminal C and foreign language right-hand side γ: $\mathbf{r}_1 = C \rightarrow \langle \gamma, \alpha_1, \sim_1, \vec{\varphi}_1 \rangle$ and $\mathbf{r}_2 = C \rightarrow \langle \gamma, \alpha_2, \sim_2, \vec{\varphi}_2 \rangle$, we pivot over γ and create a paraphrase rule $\mathbf{r}_p$: $\mathbf{r}_p = C \rightarrow \langle \alpha_1, \alpha_2, \sim, \vec{\varphi} \rangle$. We estimate the cost for $\mathbf{r}_p$ following Equation 1.

2.3 Task-Based Evaluation

Sharing its SCFG formalism permits us to re-use much of SMT's machinery for paraphrasing applications, including decoding and minimum error rate training. This allows us to easily tackle a variety of monolingual text-to-text generation tasks, which can be cast as sentential paraphrasing with task-specific constraints or goals.

For our evaluation, we apply our paraphrase system to sentence compression. However, to successfully use paraphrases for sentence compression, we need to adapt the system to suit the task. We introduce a four-point adaptation scheme for text-to-text generation via paraphrases, suggesting:

- The use *task-targeted features* that capture information pertinent to the text transformation. For sentence compression the features include word count and length-difference features.
- An *objective function* that takes into account the contraints imposed by the task. We use PRÉCIS, an augmentation of the BLEU metric, which introduces a verbosity penalty.
- *Development data* that represents the precise transformations we seek to model. We use a set of human-made example compressions mined from translation references.
- Optionally, *grammar augmentations* that allow for the incorporation of effects that the learned paraphrase grammar cannot capture. We experimented with automatically generated deletion rules.

Applying the above adaptations to our generic paraphraser (PP), quickly yields a sentence compression system that performs on par with a state-of-the-art integer linear programming-based (ILP) compression system (Clarke and Lapata, 2008). As Table 2 shows, human evaluation results suggest that our system outperforms the contrast system in meaning retention. However, it suffers losses in grammaticality. Figure 2 shows an example derivation produced as a result of applying our paraphrase rules in the decoding process.

3 Integrating Monolingual Distributional Similarity into Bilingually Extracted Paraphrases

Distributional similarity-based methods (Lin and Pantel, 2001; Bhagat and Ravichandran, 2008) rely on the assumption that similar expressions appear in similar contexts – a signal that is orthogonal to bilingual pivot information we have considered thus far. However, the monolingual distributional signal is noisy: it suffers from problems such as mistaking cousin expressions or antonyms (such as $\langle rise, fall\rangle$ or $\langle boy, girl\rangle$) for paraphrases. We circumvent this issue by starting with a paraphrase grammar extracted from bilingual data and *reranking* it with information based on distributional similarity (Ganitkevitch et al., 2012).

3.1 Distributional Similarity

In order to compute the similarity of two expressions e_1 and e_2, their respective occurrences across a corpus are aggregated in context vectors $\vec{c}_1$ and $\vec{c}_2$. The $\vec{c}_i$ are typically vectors in a high-dimensional feature space with features like counts for words seen within a window of an e_i. For parsed data more sophisticated features based on syntax and dependency structure around an occurrence are possible. The comparison of e_1 and e_2 is then made by computing the cosine similarity between $\vec{c}_1$ and $\vec{c}_2$.

Over large corpora the context vectors for even moderately frequent e_i can grow unmanageably large. Locality sensitive hashing provides a way of dealing with this problem: instead of retaining the explicit sparse high-dimensional $\vec{c}_i$, we use a random projection $h(\cdot)$ to convert them into compact bit signatures in a dense b-dimensional boolean space in which approximate similarity calculation is possible.

3.2 Integrating Similarity with Syntactic Paraphrases

In order to incorporate distributional similarity information into the paraphrasing system, we need to calculate similarity scores for the paraphrastic SCFG rules in our grammar. For rules with purely lexical right-hand sides e_1 and e_2 this is a simple task, and the similarity score $sim(e_1, e_2)$ can be directly included in the rule's feature vector $\vec{\varphi}$. However, if e_1 and e_2 are long, their occurrences become sparse and their similarity can no longer be reliably estimated. In our case, the right-hand sides of our rules also contain non-terminal symbols and re-ordered phrases, so computing a similarity score is not straightforward.

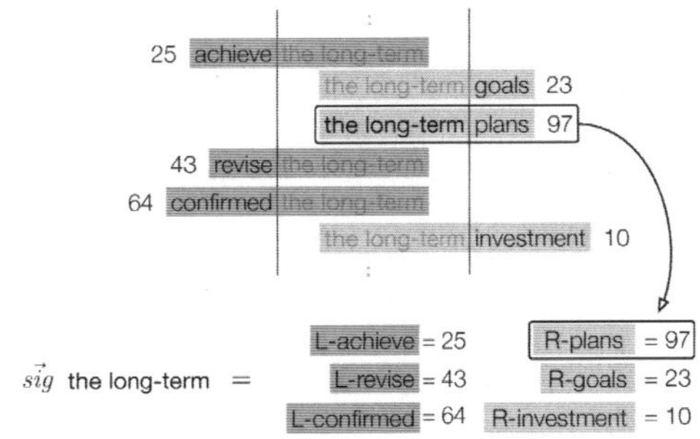

Figure 3: An example of the n-gram feature extraction on an n-gram corpus. Here, "the long-term" is seen preceded by "revise" (43 times) and followed by "plans" (97 times).

Our solution is to decompose the discontinuous patterns that make up the right-hand sides of a rule $\mathbf{r}$ into pairs of contiguous phrases, for which we then look up distributional signatures and compute similarity scores. To avoid comparing unrelated pairs, we require the phrase pairs to be consistent with a token alignment $\mathbf{a}$, defined and computed analogously to word alignments in machine translation.

3.3 Data Sets and Types of Distributional Signatures

We investigate the impact of the data and feature set used to construct distributional signatures. In particular we contrast two approaches: a large collection of distributional signatures with a relatively simple feature set, and a much smaller set of signatures with a rich, syntactically informed feature set.

The larger *n-gram model* is drawn from a web-scale n-gram corpus (Brants and Franz, 2006; Lin et al., 2010). Figure 3 illustrates this feature extraction approach. The resulting collection comprises distributional signatures for the 200 million most frequent 1-to-4-grams in the n-gram corpus.

For the syntactically informed model, we use the constituency and dependency parses provided in the Annotated Gigaword corpus (Napoles et al., 2012). Figure 4 illustrates this model's feature extraction for an example phrase occurrence. Using this method we extract distributional signatures for over 12 million 1-to-4-gram phrases.

3.4 Evaluation

For evaluation, we follow the task-based approach taken in Section 2 and apply the similarity-scored

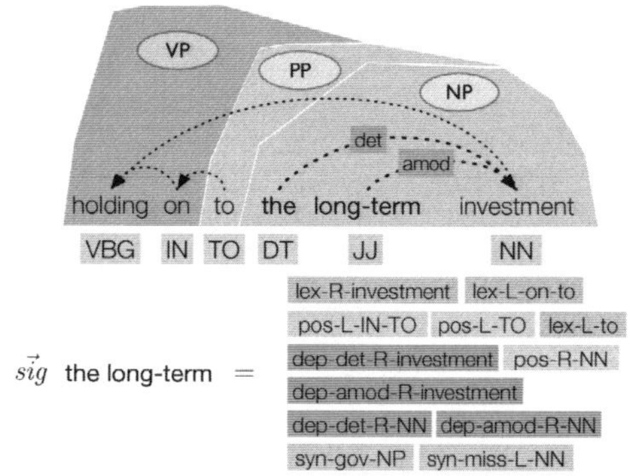

Figure 4: An example of the syntactic feature-set. The phrase "the long-term" is annotated with position-aware lexical and part-of-speech n-gram features, labeled dependency links, and features derived from the phrase's CCG label (NP/NN).

paraphrases to sentence compression. The distributional similarity scores are incorporated into the paraphrasing system as additional rule features into the log-linear model. The task-targeted parameter tuning thus results in a reranking of the rules that takes into consideration, the distributional information, bilingual alignment-based paraphrase probabilities, and compression-centric features.

Table 2 shows comparison of the bilingual baseline paraphrase grammar (PP), the reranked grammars based on signatures extracted from the Google n-grams (n-gram), the richer signatures drawn from Annotated Gigaword (Syntax), and Clarke and Lapata (2008)'s compression system (ILP). In both cases, the inclusion of distributional similarity information results in significantly better output grammaticality and meaning retention. Despite its lower coverage (12 versus 200 million phrases), the syntactic distributional similarity outperforms the simpler Google n-gram signatures.

3.5 PPDB

To facilitate a more widespread use of paraphrases, we release a collection of ranked paraphrases obtained by the methods outlined in Sections 2 and 3 to the public (Ganitkevitch et al., 2013).

4 Paraphrasing with Natural Logic

In the previously derived paraphrase grammar it is assumed that all rules imply the semantic equivalence of two textual expressions. The varying degrees of confidence our system has in this relationship are evidenced by the paraphrase probabilities and similarity scores. However, the grammar can also contain rules that in fact represent a range of semantic relationships, including hypernym- hyponym relationships, such as *India – this country*.

To better model such cases we propose an annotation of each paraphrase rule with *explicit relation labels* based on natural logic. Natural logic (MacCartney, 2009) defines a set of pairwise relations between textual expressions, such as equivalence ($\equiv$), forward ($\sqsubset$) and backward ($\sqsupset$) entailment, negation $\wedge$) and others. These relations can be used to not only detect semantic equivalence, but also infer entailment. Our resulting system will be able to tackle tasks like RTE, where the more a fine-grained resolution of semantic relationships is crucial to performance.

We favor a classification-based approach to this problem: for each pair of paraphrases in the grammar, we extract a feature vector that aims to capture information about the semantic relationship in the rule. Using a manually annotated development set of paraphrases with relation labels, we train a classifier to discriminate between the different natural logic relations.

We propose to leverage both labeled and unlabeled data resources to extract useful features for the classification. Annotated resources like WordNet can be used to derive a catalog of word and phrase pairs with known entailment relationships, for instance $\langle India, country, \sqsubset\rangle$. Using word alignments between our paraphrase pairs, we can establish what portions of a pair have labels in WordNet and retain corresponding features.

To leverage unlabeled data, we propose extending our notion of distributional similarity. Previously, we used cosine similarity to compare the signatures of two phrases. However, cosine similarity is a symmetric measure, and it is unlikely to prove helpful for determining the (asymmetric) entailment directionality of a paraphrase pair (i.e. whether it is a hypo- or hypernym relation). We therefore propose to extract a variety of asymmetric similarity features from distributional contexts. Specifically, we seek a measure that compares both the similarity and the "breadth" of two vectors. Assuming that wider breadth implies a hypernym, i.e. a $\sqsubset$-entailment, the scores produced by such a measure can be highly

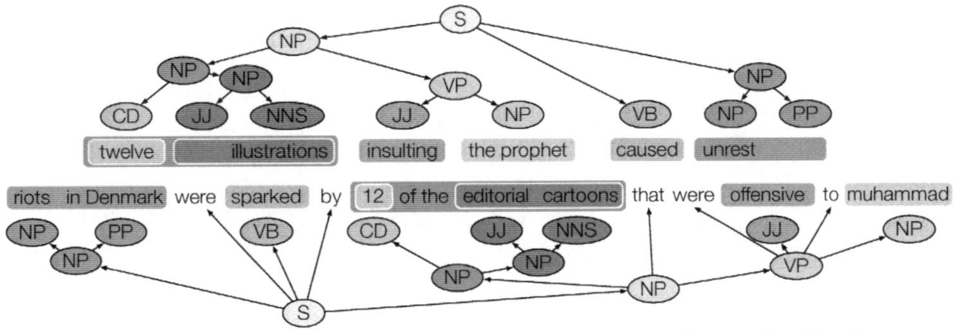

Paraphrase rules			Entailment classification		
$CD \rightarrow$	twelve	12	twelve	$\equiv$	12
$JJ \rightarrow$	ϵ	editorial	ϵ	$\sqsupset$	editorial
$NNS \rightarrow$	illustrations	cartoons	illustrations	$\sqsupset$	cartoons
$JJ \rightarrow$	insulting	offensive	insulting	$\equiv / \sqsubset$	offensive
$NP \rightarrow$	the prophet	muhammad	the prophet	$\equiv$	muhammad
$VB \rightarrow$	caused	sparked	caused	$\sqsupset$	sparked
$NP \rightarrow$	unrest	riots	unrest	$\sqsupset$	riots
$PP \rightarrow$	ϵ	in Denmark	ϵ	$\sqsupset$	in Denmark
$NP \rightarrow$	$CD(\equiv)\ NNS(\sqsupset)$	$CD(\equiv)$ of the $NNS(\sqsupset)$	twelve illustrations	$\sqsupset$	12 of the cartoons

Figure 5: Our system will use synchronous parsing and paraphrase grammars to perform natural language inference. Each paraphrase transformation will be classified with a natural logic entailment relation. These will be joined bottom-up, as illustrated by the last rule, where the join of the smaller constituents $\equiv \bowtie \sqsupset$ results in $\sqsupset$ for the larger phrase pairs. This process will be propagated up the trees to determine if the hypothesis can be inferred from the premise.

informative for our classification problem. Asymmetric measures like Tversky indices (Tolias et al., 2001) appear well-suited to the problem. We will investigate application of Tversky indices to our distributional signatures and their usefulness for entailment relation classification.

4.1 Task-Based Evaluation

We propose evaluating the resulting system on textual entailment recognition. To do this, we cast the RTE task as a synchronous parsing problem, as illustrated in Figure 5. We will extend the notion of synchronous parsing towards resolving entailments, and define and implement a compositional join operator $\bowtie$ to compute entailment relations over synchronous derivations from the individual rule entailments.

While the assumption of a synchronous parse structure is likely to be valid for translations and paraphrases, we do not expect it to straightforwardly hold for entailment recognition. We will thus investigate the limits of the synchronous assumption over RTE data. Furthermore, to expand the system's coverage in a first step, we propose a simple relaxation of the synchronousness requirement via entailment-less "glue rules." These rules, similar to out-of-vocabulary rules in translation, will allow us to include potentially unrelated or unrecognized portions of the input into the synchronous parse.

5 Conclusion

We have described an extension of the state of the art in paraphrasing in a number of important ways: we leverage large bilingual data sets to extract linguistically expressive high-coverage paraphrases based on an SCFG formalism. On an example text-to-text generation task, sentence compression, we show that an easily adapted paraphrase system achieves state of the art meaning retention. Further, we include a complementary data source, monolingual corpora, to augment the quality of the previously obtained paraphrase grammar. The resulting system is shown to perform significantly better than the purely bilingual paraphrases, in both meaning retention and grammaticality, achieving results on par with the state of the art. Finally, we propose an extension of SCFG-based paraphrasing towards a more fine grained semantic representation using a classification-based approach. In extending the synchronous parsing methodology, we outline the expansion of the paraphraser towards a system capable of tackling entailment recognition tasks.

Acknowledgements

The ideas described in this paper were developed in collaboration with Benjamin Van Durme and Chris Callison-Burch. This material is based on research sponsored by the NSF under grant IIS-1249516 and DARPA under agreement number FA8750-13-2-0017 (the DEFT program). The U.S. Government is authorized to reproduce and distribute reprints for Governmental purposes. The views and conclusions contained in this publication are those of the authors and should not be interpreted as representing official policies or endorsements of DARPA, the NSF, or the U.S. Government.

References

Alfred V. Aho and Jeffrey D. Ullman. 1972. *The Theory of Parsing, Translation, and Compiling*. Prentice Hall.

Colin Bannard and Chris Callison-Burch. 2005. Paraphrasing with bilingual parallel corpora. In *Proceedings of ACL*.

Rahul Bhagat and Deepak Ravichandran. 2008. Large scale acquisition of paraphrases for learning surface patterns. In *Proceedings of ACL/HLT*.

Thorsten Brants and Alex Franz. 2006. Web 1T 5-gram version 1.

Peter Brown, John Cocke, Stephen Della Pietra, Vincent Della Pietra, Frederick Jelinek, Robert Mercer, and Paul Poossin. 1990. A statistical approach to language translation. *Computational Linguistics*, 16(2), June.

Chris Callison-Burch. 2007. *Paraphrasing and Translation*. Ph.D. thesis, University of Edinburgh, Edinburgh, Scotland.

Chris Callison-Burch. 2008. Syntactic constraints on paraphrases extracted from parallel corpora. In *Proceedings of EMNLP*.

David Chiang. 2005. A hierarchical phrase-based model for statistical machine translation. In *Proceedings of ACL*.

James Clarke and Mirella Lapata. 2008. Global inference for sentence compression: An integer linear programming approach. *Journal of Artificial Intelligence Research*, 31:273–381.

Juri Ganitkevitch, Chris Callison-Burch, Courtney Napoles, and Benjamin Van Durme. 2011. Learning sentential paraphrases from bilingual parallel corpora for text-to-text generation. In *Proceedings of EMNLP*.

Juri Ganitkevitch, Benjamin Van Durme, and Chris Callison-Burch. 2012. Monolingual distributional similarity for text-to-text generation. In *Proceedings of *SEM*. Association for Computational Linguistics.

Juri Ganitkevitch, Chris Callison-Burch, and Benjamin Van Durme. 2013. Ppdb: The paraphrase database. In *Proceedings of HLT/NAACL*.

Philipp Koehn, Franz Josef Och, and Daniel Marcu. 2003. Statistical phrase-based translation. In *Proceedings of HLT/NAACL*.

Dekang Lin and Patrick Pantel. 2001. Discovery of inference rules from text. *Natural Language Engineering*.

Dekang Lin, Kenneth Church, Heng Ji, Satoshi Sekine, David Yarowsky, Shane Bergsma, Kailash Patil, Emily Pitler, Rachel Lathbury, Vikram Rao, Kapil Dalwani, and Sushant Narsale. 2010. New tools for web-scale n-grams. In *Proceedings of LREC*.

Bill MacCartney. 2009. *Natural language inference*. Ph.D. thesis, Stanford University.

Nitin Madnani and Bonnie Dorr. 2010. Generating phrasal and sentential paraphrases: A survey of data-driven methods. *Computational Linguistics*, 36(3):341–388.

Courtney Napoles, Matt Gormley, and Benjamin Van Durme. 2012. Annotated gigaword. In *Proceedings of AKBC-WEKEX 2012*.

Yannis A. Tolias, Stavros M. Panas, and Lefteri H. Tsoukalas. 2001. Generalized fuzzy indices for similarity matching. *Fuzzy Sets and Systems*, 120(2):255–270.

Domain-Independent Captioning of Domain-Specific Images

Rebecca Mason
Brown Laboratory for Linguistic Information Processing (BLLIP)
Brown University, Providence, RI 02912
rebecca@cs.brown.edu

Abstract

Automatically describing visual content is an extremely difficult task, with hard AI problems in Computer Vision (CV) and Natural Language Processing (NLP) at its core. Previous work relies on supervised visual recognition systems to determine the content of images. These systems require massive amounts of hand-labeled data for training, so the number of visual classes that can be recognized is typically very small. We argue that these approaches place unrealistic limits on the kinds of images that can be captioned, and are unlikely to produce captions which reflect human interpretations.

We present a framework for image caption generation that does not rely on visual recognition systems, which we have implemented on a dataset of online shopping images and product descriptions. We propose future work to improve this method, and extensions for other domains of images and natural text.

1 Introduction

As the number of images on the web continues to increase, the task of automatically describing images becomes especially important. Image captions can provide background information about what is seen in the image, can improve accessibility of websites for visually-impaired users, and can improve image retrieval by providing text to search user queries against. Typically, online search engines rely on collocated textual information to resolve queries, rather than analyzing visual content directly. Likewise, earlier image captioning research from the Natural Language Processing (NLP) community use collocated information such as news articles or GPS coordinates, to decide what information to include in the generated caption (Deschacht and Moens, 2007; Aker and Gaizauskas, 2010; Fan et al., 2010; Feng and Lapata, 2010a).

However, in some instances visual recognition is necessary because collocated information is missing, irrelevant, or unreliable. Recognition is a classic Computer Vision (CV) problem including tasks such as recognizing instances of object classes in images (such as `car`, `cat`, or `sofa`); classifying images by scene (such as `beach` or `forest`); or detecting attributes in an image (such as `wooden` or `feathered`). Recent works in image caption generation represent visual content via the output of trained recognition systems for a pre-defined set of visual classes. They then use linguistic models to correct noisy initial detections (Kulkarni et al., 2011; Yang et al., 2011), and generate more natural-sounding text (Li et al., 2011; Mitchell et al., 2012; Kuznetsova et al., 2012).

A key problem with this approach is that it assumes that image captioning is a grounding problem, with language acting only as labels for visual meaning. One good reason to challenge this assumption is that it imposes unrealistic constraints on the kinds of images that can be automatically described. Previous work only recognizes a limited number of visual classes – typically no more than a few dozen in total – because training CV systems requires a huge amount of hand-annotated data. For example, the PASCAL VOC dataset[1] has 11,530 training im-

[1]http://pascallin.ecs.soton.ac.uk/

Proceedings of the NAACL HLT 2013 Student Research Workshop, pages 69–76,
Atlanta, Georgia, 13 June 2013.

ages with 27,450 labeled objects, in order to learn only 20 object classes. Since training visual recognition systems is such a burden, "general-domain" image captioning datasets are limited by the current technology. For example, the SBU-Flickr dataset (Ordonez et al., 2011), which contains 1 million images and captions, is built by first querying Flickr using a pre-defined set of queries, then further filtering to remove instances where the caption does not contain at least two words belonging to their term list. Furthermore, detections are too noisy to generate a good caption for the majority of images. For example, Kuznetsova et al. (2012) select their test set according to which images receive the most confident visual object detection scores.

We instead direct our attention to the *domain-specific* image captioning task, assuming that we know a general object or scene category for the query image, and that we have access to a dataset of images and captions from the same domain. While some techniques may be unrealistic in assuming that high-quality collocated text is always available, assuming that there is no collocated information at all is equally unrealistic. Data sources such as file names, website text, Facebook likes, and web searches all provide clues to the content of an image. Even an image file by itself carries metadata on where and when it was taken, and the camera settings used to take it. Since visual recognition is much easier for domain-specific tasks, there is more potential for natural language researchers to do research that will impact the greater community.

Finally, labeling visual content is often not enough to provide an adequate caption. The meaning of an image to a user is more than just listing the objects in the image, and can even change for different users. This problem is commonly known as "bridging the semantic gap":

> "The semantic gap is the lack of coincidence between the information that one can extract from the visual data and the interpretation that the same data have for a user in a given situation. A linguistic description is almost always contextual, whereas an image may live by itself." (Smeulders et al., 2000)

General-domain models of caption generation fail to capture context because they assume that all the relevant information has been provided in the image. However, training models on data from the same domain gives *implicit* context about what information should be provided in the generated text.

This thesis proposes a framework for image captioning that does not require supervision in the form of hand-labeled examples. We train a topic model on a corpus of images and captions in the same domain, in order to jointly learn image features and natural language descriptions. The trained topic model is used to estimate the likelihood of words appearing in a caption, given an unseen query image. We then use these likelihoods to rewrite an extracted human-written caption to accurately describe the query image. We have implemented our framework using a dataset of online shopping images and captions, and propose to extend this model to other domains, including natural images.

2 Framework

In this section, we provide an overview of our image captioning framework, as it is currently implemented. As shown in Figure 1, the data that we use are a set of images and captions in a specific domain, and a query image that is from the same domain, but is not included in the training data. The training data is used in two ways: for **sentence extraction** from the captions of training images that are visually similar to the query image overall; and for training a **topic model** of individual words and local image features, in order to capture fine-grained details. Finally, a **sentence compression** algorithm is used to remove details from the extracted captions that do not fit the query image.

The work that we have done so far has been implemented using the Attribute Discovery Dataset (Berg et al., 2010), a publicly available dataset of shopping images and product descriptions.[2] Here, we run our framework on the women's shoes section, which has over 14000 images and captions, representing a wide variety of attributes for texture, shapes, materials, colors, and other visual qualities. The women's shoes section is formally split

challenges/VOC/

[2]http://tamaraberg.com/attributesDataset/index.html

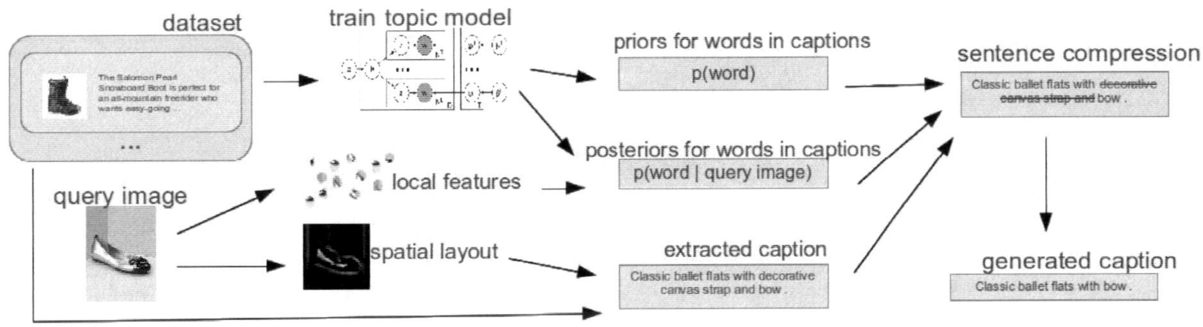

Figure 1: Overview of our framework for image caption generation.

into ten subcategories, such as wedding shoes, sneakers, and rainboots. However, many of the subcategories contain multiple visually distinct kinds of shoes. We do not make use of the subcategories, instead we group all of the categories of shoe images together. The shoes in the images are mostly posed against solid color backgrounds, while the captions have much more variability in length and linguistic quality.

For our thesis work, we intend to extend our current framework to different domains of data, including natural images. However, it is important to point out that no part of the framework as it is currently implemented is specific to describing shoes or shopping images. This will be described in Section 4.

2.1 Sentence Extraction

GIST (Oliva and Torralba, 2001) is a *global* image descriptor which describes how gradients are oriented in different regions of an image. It is commonly used for classifying background scenes in images, however images in the Attribute Discovery Dataset do not have "backgrounds" per se. Instead, we treat the overall shape of the object as the "scene" and extract a caption sentence using GIST nearest neighbors between the query image and the images in the training set. Because similar objects and attributes tend to appear in similar scenes, we expect that at least some of the extracted caption will describe local attributes that are also in the query image. The rest of our framework finds and removes the parts of the extracted caption that are not accurate to the query image.

2.2 Topic Model

Image captions often act as more than labels of visual content. Some visual ideas can be described using several different words, while others are typically not described at all. Likewise, some words describe background information that is not shown visually, or contextual information that is interpreted by the user. Rather than modeling images and text such that one generates the other, we a topic model based on LDA (Blei et al., 2003) where both an image and its caption are generated by a shared latent distribution of topics.

Previous work by (Feng and Lapata, 2010b) shows that topic models where image features or regions generate text features (such as Blei and Jordan (2003)) are not appropriate for modeling images with captions or other collocated text. We use a topic model designed for multi-lingual data, specifically the Polylingual Topic Model (Mimno et al., 2009). This model was developed for correlated documents in different languages that are topically similar, but are not direct translations, such as Wikipedia or news articles in different languages. We train the topic model with images and text as two languages. For query images, we estimate the topic distribution that generated just the image, and then In the model, images and their captions are represented using *bag-of-words*, a commonly-used technique for document representation in both CV and NLP research. The textual features are non-function words in the model, including words that describe specific objects or attributes (such as boot, snake-skin, buckle, and metallic) in addition to words that describe more abstract attributes and affordances (such as professional, flirty, support,

Original: Go all-out glam in the shimmering Dyeables Roxie sandals. Metallic faux leather upper in a dress thong sandal style with a round open toe. ...	**Original:** Find the softness of shearling combined with support in this clog slipper. The cork footbed mimics the foot's natural shape, offering arch support, while a flexible outsole flexes with your steps and resists slips. ...	**Original:** Perforated leather with cap toe and bow detail.
Extracted: Shimmering snake-embossed leather upper in a slingback evening dress sandal style with a round open toe .	**Extracted:** This sporty sneaker clog keeps foot cool and comfortable and fully supported.	**Extracted:** Italian patent leather peep-toe ballet flat with a signature tailored grosgrain bow .
System: Shimmering upper in a slingback evening dress sandal style with a round open toe .	**System:** This clog keeps foot comfortable and supported.	**System:** leather ballet flat with a signature tailored grosgrain bow .

Table 1: Some examples of shoes images from the Attribute Discovery Dataset and performance with our image captioning model. Left: Correctly removes explicitly visual feature "snake-embossed leather" from extraction; leaves in correct visual attributes "shimmering", "slingback", and "round open toe". Center: Extracted sentence with some contextually visual attributes; the model correctly infers that "sporty" and "cool" are not likely given an image of a wool bedroom slipper, but "comfortable" and "supported" are likely because of the visible cork soles. Right: Extracted sentence with some non-visual attributes; model removes "Italian" but keeps "signature tailored".

and `waterproof`). For "image words", we compute features at several points in the image such as the color values of pixels, the angles of edges or corners, and response to various filters, and cluster them into discrete image words. However, the information that an image word conveys is very different than the information conveyed in a text word, so models which require direct correspondence between features in the two modalities would not be appropriate here.

We train the topic model with images and text as two languages. We estimate the probabilities of textual words given a query image by first estimating the topic distribution that generated the image, and then using the same distribution to find the probabilities of textual words given the query image. However, we also perform an annotation task similarly to Feng and Lapata (2010b), in order to evaluate the topic model on its own. Our method has a 30-35% improvement in finding words from the held-out image caption, compared to previous methods and baselines.

2.3 Sentence Compression via Caption Generation

We describe an ILP for caption generation, drawing inspiration from sentence compression work by Clarke and Lapata (2008). The ILP has three inputs: the extracted caption; the prior probabilities words appearing in captions, $p(w)$; and their posterior probabilities of words appearing in captions given the query image, $p(w|query)$. The latter is estimated using the topic model we have just described. The output of the ILP is a compressed image caption where the inaccurate words have been deleted.

Objective: The formal ILP objective[3] is to maximize a weighted linear combination of two measures. The first we define as $\sum_{i=1}^{n} \delta_i \cdot I(w_i)$, where $w_i, ..., w_n$ are words in the extracted caption, δ_i is a binary decision variable which is true if we include w_i in the compressed output, and $I(w_i)$ is a score for the accuracy of each word. For non-function words,

[3]To formulate this problem as a linear program, the probabilities are actually log probabilities, but we omit the logs in this paper to save space.

$I(w_i) = p(w|query) - p(w)$, which can have a positive or negative value. We do not use $p(w_i|query)$ directly in order to distinguish between cases where $p(w_i|query)$ is low because w_i is inaccurate, and cases where $p(w_i|query)$ is low because $p(w_i)$ is low generally. Function words do not affect the accuracy of the generated caption, so $I(w_i) = 0$.

The second measure in the objective is a trigram language model, described in detail in Clarke (2008). In the original sentence compression task, the language model is a component as it naturally prefers shorter output sentences. However, our objective is not to generate a shorter caption, but to generate a more accurate caption. However, we still include the language model in the objective, with a weighting factor ϵ, as it helps remove unnecessary function words and help reduce the search space of possible sentence compressions.

Constraints: The ILP constraints include sequential constraints to ensure the mathematical validity of the model, and syntactic constraints that ensure the grammatical correctness of the compressed sentence. We do not have space here to describe all of the constraints, but basically, using the "semantic head" version of the headfinder from Collins (1999), we constrain that the head word of the sentence and the head word of the sentence's object cannot be deleted, and for any word that we include in the output sentence, we must include its head word as well. We also have constraints that define valid use of coordinating conjunctions and punctuation.

We evaluate generated captions using automatic metrics such as BLEU (Papineni et al., 2002) and ROUGE (Lin, 2004). These metrics are commonly used in summarization and translation research and have been previously used in image captioning research to compare automatically generated captions to human-written captions for each image (Ordonez et al., 2011; Yang et al., 2011; Kuznetsova et al., 2012). Although human-written captions may use synonyms to describe a visual object or attribute, or even describe entirely different attributes than what is described in the generated captions, computing the automatic metrics over a large test set finds statistically significant improvements in the accuracy of the extracted and compressed captions over extraction alone.

For our proposed work (Section 4), we also plan to perform manual evaluations of our captions based on their content and language quality. However, cross-system comparisons would be more difficult because our method uses an entirely different kind of data. In order to compare our work to related methods (Section 3), we would have to train for visual recognition systems for hundreds of visual attributes, which would mean having to hand-label the entire dataset.

3 Related Work in Image Captioning

In addition to visual recognition, caption generation is a very challenging problem. In some approaches, sentences are constructed using templates or grammar rules, where content words are selected according to the output of visual recognition systems (Kulkarni et al., 2011; Yang et al., 2011; Mitchell et al., 2012). Function words, as well as words like verbs and prepositions which are difficult to recognize visually, may be selected using a language model trained on non-visual text. There is also similar work that uses large-scale ngram models to make the generated output sound more natural (Li et al., 2011).

In other approaches, captions are extracted in whole or in part from similar images in a database. For example, Farhadi et al. (2010) and Ordonez et al. (2011) build semantic representations for visual content of query images, and extract captions from database images with similar content. Kuznetsova et al. (2012) extract phrases corresponding to classes of objects and scenes detected in the query image, and combine extracted phrases into a single sentence. Our work is different than these approaches, because we directly measure how visually relevant individual words are, rather than only using visual similarity to extract sentences or phrases.

Our method is most similar to that of Feng and Lapata (2010a), who generate captions for news images. Like them, we train an LDA-like model on both images and text to find latent topics that generate both. However, their model requires both an image and collocated text (a news article) to estimate the topic distribution for an unseen image, while our topic model only needs related text for the training data. They also use the news article to help generate captions, which means that optimizing their generated output for content and grammaticality is a much easier problem. Although their model combines phrases and n-grams from different sentences to form an image caption, they only consider the text from a single news article for extraction, and they can assume that the text is mostly accurate and relevant to the content of the image.

In this sense, our method is more like Kuznetsova et al. (2012), which also uses an Integer Linear Program (ILP) to rapidly optimize how well their generated caption fits the content of the image model. However, it is easier to get coherent image captions from our model since we are not combining parts of sentences from multiple sources. Since we build our output from extracted sentences, not phrases, our ILP requires fewer grammaticality and coherence constraints than it would for building new sentences from scratch. We also model how relevant each individual word is to the query image, while they extract phrases based on visual similarity of detected objects in the images.

4 Proposed Work

One clear direction for future work is to extend our image captioning framework to natural images. By "natural images" we refer to images of everyday scenes seen by people, unlike the shopping images, where objects tend to be posed in similar positions against plain backgrounds. Instead of domains such as handbags and shoes, we propose to cluster the training data based on visual scene domains such as mountains, beaches, and living rooms. We are particularly interested in the scene attributes and classifiers by Patterson and Hays (2012) which builds an attribute-based taxonomy of scene types using crowd-sourcing, rather than categorical scene types which are typically used.

Visual recognition is generally much more difficult in natural scenes than in posed images, since lighting and viewpoints are not consistent, and objects may be occluded by other objects or truncated by the edge of the image. However, we are optimistic because we do not need to solve the *general* visual recognition task, since our model only learns how visual objects and attributes appear in specific domains of scenes, a much easier problem. Additionally, the space of likely objects and attributes to detect is limited by what typically appears in that type of scene. Finally, we can use the fact that our image captioning method is not grounded in our favor, and assume that if an object is partially occluded or truncated in an image, than it is less likely that the photographer considered that object to be interesting, so it is not as important whether that object is described in the caption or not.

Finally, there is also much that could be done to improve the text generation component on its own. Our framework currently extracts only a single caption sentence to compress, while recent work in summarization has focused on the problem of learning how to jointly extract and compress (Martins and Smith, 2009; Berg-Kirkpatrick et al., 2011). Since a poor extraction choice can make finding an accurate compression impossible, we should also study different methods of extraction to learn about what kinds of features are most likely to help us find good sentences. As mentioned in Section 2.1, we have already found that global feature descriptors are better than bag of image word descriptors for extracting sentences to use in image caption compressions in the shopping dataset. As we extend our framework to other domains of images, we are interested in finding whether scene-based descriptors and classifiers in general are better at finding good sentences than local descriptors, and whether there is a connection between region and phrase-based detectors correlating better with sentence and phrase-length text, while local image descriptors are more related to single words. Finding patterns like this in visual text in general would be helpful for many other tasks besides image captioning.

References

Ahmet Aker and Robert Gaizauskas. 2010. Generating image descriptions using dependency relational patterns. In *Proceedings of the 48th Annual Meeting of the Association for Computational Linguistics*, ACL '10, pages 1250–1258, Stroudsburg, PA, USA. Association for Computational Linguistics.

Tamara L. Berg, Alexander C. Berg, and Jonathan Shih. 2010. Automatic attribute discovery and characterization from noisy web data. In *Proceedings of the 11th European conference on Computer vision: Part I*, ECCV'10, pages 663–676, Berlin, Heidelberg. Springer-Verlag.

Taylor Berg-Kirkpatrick, Dan Gillick, and Dan Klein. 2011. Jointly learning to extract and compress. In *Proceedings of the 49th Annual Meeting of the Association for Computational Linguistics: Human Language Technologies - Volume 1*, HLT '11, pages 481–490, Stroudsburg, PA, USA. Association for Computational Linguistics.

David M. Blei and Michael I. Jordan. 2003. Modeling annotated data. In *Proceedings of the 26th annual international ACM SIGIR conference on Research and development in informaion retrieval*, SIGIR '03, pages 127–134, New York, NY, USA. ACM.

David M. Blei, Andrew Y. Ng, and Michael I. Jordan. 2003. Latent dirichlet allocation. *J. Mach. Learn. Res.*, 3:993–1022, March.

James Clarke and Mirella Lapata. 2008. Global inference for sentence compression an integer linear programming approach. *J. Artif. Int. Res.*, 31(1):399–429, March.

James Clarke. 2008. *Global Inference for Sentence Compression: An Integer Linear Programming Approach.* Dissertation, University of Edinburgh.

Michael John Collins. 1999. *Head-driven statistical models for natural language parsing*. Ph.D. thesis, Philadelphia, PA, USA. AAI9926110.

Koen Deschacht and Marie-Francine Moens. 2007. Text analysis for automatic image annotation. In *ACL*, volume 45, page 1000.

Xin Fan, Ahmet Aker, Martin Tomko, Philip Smart, Mark Sanderson, and Robert Gaizauskas. 2010. Automatic image captioning from the web for gps photographs. In *Proceedings of the international conference on Multimedia information retrieval*, MIR '10, pages 445–448, New York, NY, USA. ACM.

Ali Farhadi, Mohsen Hejrati, Mohammad Amin Sadeghi, Peter Young, Cyrus Rashtchian, Julia Hockenmaier, and David Forsyth. 2010. Every picture tells a story: generating sentences from images. In *Proceedings of the 11th European conference on Computer vision: Part IV*, ECCV'10, pages 15–29, Berlin, Heidelberg. Springer-Verlag.

Yansong Feng and Mirella Lapata. 2010a. How many words is a picture worth? automatic caption generation for news images. In *Proceedings of the 48th Annual Meeting of the Association for Computational Linguistics*, ACL '10, pages 1239–1249, Stroudsburg, PA, USA. Association for Computational Linguistics.

Yansong Feng and Mirella Lapata. 2010b. Topic models for image annotation and text illustration. In *HLT-NAACL*, pages 831–839.

Girish Kulkarni, Visruth Premraj, Sagnik Dhar, Siming Li, Yejin Choi, Alexander C. Berg, and Tamara L. Berg. 2011. Baby talk: Understanding and generating simple image descriptions. In *CVPR*, pages 1601–1608.

Polina Kuznetsova, Vicente Ordonez, Alexander C. Berg, Tamara L. Berg, and Yejin Choi. 2012. Collective generation of natural image descriptions. In *ACL*.

Siming Li, Girish Kulkarni, Tamara L. Berg, Alexander C. Berg, and Yejin Choi. 2011. Composing simple image descriptions using web-scale n-grams. In *Proceedings of the Fifteenth Conference on Computational Natural Language Learning*, CoNLL '11, pages 220–228, Stroudsburg, PA, USA. Association for Computational Linguistics.

Chin-Yew Lin. 2004. Rouge: A package for automatic evaluation of summaries. In Stan Szpakowicz Marie-Francine Moens, editor, *Text Summarization Branches Out: Proceedings of the ACL-04 Workshop*, pages 74–81, Barcelona, Spain, July. Association for Computational Linguistics.

André F. T. Martins and Noah A. Smith. 2009. Summarization with a joint model for sentence extraction and compression. In *Proceedings of the Workshop on Integer Linear Programming for Natural Langauge Processing*, ILP '09, pages 1–9, Stroudsburg, PA, USA. Association for Computational Linguistics.

David Mimno, Hanna M. Wallach, Jason Naradowsky, David A. Smith, and Andrew McCallum. 2009. Polylingual topic models. In *Proceedings of the 2009 Conference on Empirical Methods in Natural Language Processing: Volume 2 - Volume 2*, EMNLP '09, pages 880–889, Stroudsburg, PA, USA. Association for Computational Linguistics.

Margaret Mitchell, Jesse Dodge, Amit Goyal, Kota Yamaguchi, Karl Stratos, Xufeng Han, Alyssa Mensch, Alexander C. Berg, Tamara L. Berg, and Hal Daumé III. 2012. Midge: Generating image descriptions from computer vision detections. In *European Chapter of the Association for Computational Linguistics (EACL)*.

Aude Oliva and Antonio Torralba. 2001. Modeling the shape of the scene: A holistic representation of the spatial envelope. *International Journal of Computer Vision*, 42:145–175.

V. Ordonez, G. Kulkarni, and T.L. Berg. 2011. Im2text: Describing images using 1 million captioned photographs. In *NIPS*.

Kishore Papineni, Salim Roukos, Todd Ward, and Wei-Jing Zhu. 2002. Bleu: a method for automatic evaluation of machine translation. In *Proceedings of the 40th Annual Meeting on Association for Computational Linguistics*, ACL '02, pages 311–318, Stroudsburg, PA, USA. Association for Computational Linguistics.

G. Patterson and J. Hays. 2012. Sun attribute database: Discovering, annotating, and recognizing scene attributes. *2012 IEEE Conference on Computer Vision and Pattern Recognition*, 0:2751–2758.

Arnold W. M. Smeulders, Marcel Worring, Simone Santini, Amarnath Gupta, and Ramesh Jain. 2000. Content-based image retrieval at the end of the early years. *IEEE Trans. Pattern Anal. Mach. Intell.*, 22(12):1349–1380, December.

Yezhou Yang, Ching Lik Teo, Hal Daumé III, and Yiannis Aloimonos. 2011. Corpus-guided sentence generation of natural images. In *Empirical Methods in Natural Language Processing (EMNLP)*, Edinburgh, Scotland.

Helpfulness-Guided Review Summarization

Wenting Xiong
University of Pittsburgh
210 South Bouquet Street, Pittsburgh, PA 15260
wex12@cs.pitt.edu

Abstract

Review mining and summarization has been a hot topic for the past decade. A lot of effort has been devoted to aspect detection and sentiment analysis under the assumption that every review has the same utility for related tasks. However, reviews are not equally helpful as indicated by user-provided helpfulness assessment associated with the reviews. In this thesis, we propose a novel review summarization framework which summarizes review content under the supervision of automated assessment of review helpfulness. This helpfulness-guided framework can be easily adapted to traditional review summarization tasks, for a wide range of domains.

1 Introduction

Nowadays, as reviews thrive on the web, more and more people wade through these online resources to inform their own decision making. Due to the rapid growth of the review volume, the ability of automatically summarizing online reviews becomes critical to allowing people to make use of them. This makes review mining and summarization an increasingly hot topic over the past decade. Generally speaking, there are two main paradigms in review summarization. One is aspect-based opinion summarization, which aims to differentiate and summarize opinions regarding specific subject aspects. It usually involves fine-grained analysis of both review topics and review sentiment. The other is more summarization-oriented, prior work under this category either assumes a shared topic or aims to produce general summaries. In this case, the focus is the summarization, extracting salient information from reviews and organizing them properly. Compared with traditional text summarizers, sentiment-informed summarizers generally perform better as shown by human evaluation results (Carenini et al., 2006; Lerman et al., 2009).

However, one implicit assumption shared by most prior work is that all reviews are of the same utility in review summarization tasks, while reviews that comment on the same aspect and are associated with the same rating may have difference influence to users, as indicated by user-provided helpfulness assessment (e.g. "helpful" votes on Amazon.com). We believe that user-generated helpfulness votes/ratings suggest people's point of interest in review exploration. Intuitively, when users refer to online reviews for guidance, reviews that are considered helpful by more people naturally receive more attention and credit, and thus should be given more weight in review summarization. Following this intuition, we hypothesize that introducing review helpfulness information into review summarization can yield more useful review summaries.

In addition, we are also motivated by the challenges that we faced when summarizing educational peer reviews in which the review entity is also text. In the peer-review domain, traditional algorithms of identifying review aspects may suffer as reviews contain both reviewers' evaluations of a paper and reviewers' references to the paper. Such heterogeneous sources of review content bring challenges to aspect identification, and the educational perspective of peer review directly affects the characteristics of

Proceedings of the NAACL HLT 2013 Student Research Workshop, pages 77–83,
Atlanta, Georgia, 13 June 2013.

desired summaries, which has not ye been taken into consideration in any of the current summarization techniques. We expect the helpfulness assessment of peer reviews can identify important information that should be captured in peer-review summaries.

2 Related work

The proposed work is grounded in the following areas: review-helpfulness analysis, review summarization and supervised topic modeling. In this section, we will discuss existing work in the literature and explain how the proposed work relates to them.

2.1 Review-helpfulness analysis

In the literature, most researchers take a supervised approach in modeling review helpfulness. They either aggregate binary helpfulness votes for each review into a numerical score, or directly use numerical helpfulness ratings. Kim et. al (2006) took the first attempt, using regression to model review helpfulness based on various linguistic features. They reported that the combination of review length, review unigrams and product rating statistics performed best. Along this line, other studies showed the perceived review helpfulness depends not only on the review content, but also on some other factors. Ghose et. al (2008) found that the reviewer's reviewing history also matters. However, they observed that review-subjectivity, review-readability and other reviewer-related features are interchangeable for predicting review helpfulness. In addition, the empirical study on Amazon reviews conducted by Danescu-Niculescu-Mizil et. al (2009) revealed that the perceived helpfulness is also affected by how a review relates to the other reviews of the same product. However, given our goal of using review helpfulness assessment to guide summarization towards generating more useful summaries rather than to explain each individual helpfulness rating, we will ignore the interaction of helpfulness assessment among reviews of the same target.

Furthermore, the utility of features in modeling review helpfulness may vary with the review domain. Mudambi et. al (2010) showed that for product reviews, the product type moderates both the product ratings and review length on the perceived review helpfulness. For educational peer reviews, in X (2011) we showed that cognitive constructs which predict feedback implementation can further improve our helpfulness model upon general linguistic features. These findings seem to suggest that the review helpfulness model should be domain-dependent, due to the specific semantics of "helpfulness" defined in context of the domain.

2.2 Review summarization

One major paradigm of review summarization is aspect-based summarization, which is based on identifying aspects and associating opinion sentiment with them. (Although this line of work is closely related to sentiment analysis, it is not the focus of this proposed work.) While initially people use information retrieval techniques to recognize aspect terms and opinion expressions (Hu and Liu, 2004; Popescu and Etzioni, 2005), recent work seems to favor generative statistical models more (Mei et al., 2007; Lu and Zhai, 2008; Titov and McDonald, 2008b; Titov and McDonald, 2008a; Blei and McAuliffe, 2010; Brody and Elhadad, 2010; Mukherjee and Liu, 2012; Sauper and Barzilay, 2013). One typical problem with these models is that many discovered aspects are not meaningful to end-users. Some of these studies focus on distinguishing aspects in terms of sentiment variation by modeling aspects together with sentiment (Titov and McDonald, 2008a; Lu and Zhai, 2008; Mukherjee and Liu, 2012; Sauper and Barzilay, 2013). However, little attention is given to differentiating review content directly regarding their utilities in review exploration. Mukherjee and Liu (2012) attempted to address this issue by introducing user-provided aspect terms as seeds for learning review aspects, though this approach might not be easily generalized to other domains, as users' point of interest could vary with the review domain.

Another paradigm of review summarization is more summarization-oriented. In contrast, such approaches do not require the step of identifying aspects, instead, they either assume the input text share the same aspect or aim to produce general summaries. These studies are closely related to the traditional NLP task of text summarization. Generally speaking, the goal of text summarization is to retain the most important points of the input text within a shorter length. Either extractively or abstractively, one important task is to determine the informativeness of a text element. In addition to reducing information redundancy, different heuristics were proposed within the context of opinion summarization. Stoyanov and Cardie (2008) focused on identifying opinion entities (opinion, source, target) and presenting them in a structured way (templates or diagrams). Lerman et. al (2009) reported that users preferred sentiment informed summaries based on their analysis of human evaluation of various summarization models, while Kim and Zhai (2009) further considered an effective review summary as representative contrastive opinion pairs. Different from all above, Ganesan et. al (2010) represented text input as token-based graphs based on the token order in the string. They rank summary candidates by scoring paths after removing redundant information from the graph. For any summarization framework discussed above, the helpfulness of the review elements (e.g. sentences, opinion entities, or words), which can be derived from the review overall helpfulness, captures informativeness from another dimension that has not been taken into account yet.

2.3 Supervised content modeling

As review summarization is meant to help users acquire useful information effectively, what and how to summarize may vary with user needs. To discover user preferences, Ando and Ishizaki (2012) manually analyzed travel reviews to identify the most influential review sentences objectively and subjectively, while Mukherjee and Liu (2012) extract and categorize review aspects through semi-supervised modeling using user-provided seeds (categories of terms). In contrast, we are interested in using user-provided helpfulness ratings for guidance. As these helpfulness ratings are existing meta data of reviews, we will need no additional input from users. Specifically, we propose to use supervised LDA (Blei and McAuliffe, 2010) to model review content under the supervision of review helpfulness ratings. Similar approach is widely adopted in sentiment analysis, where review aspects are learned in the presence of sentiment predictions (Blei and McAuliffe, 2010; Titov and McDonald, 2008a). Furthermore, Branavan et. al (2009) showed that joint modeling of text and user annotations benefits extractive summarization. Therefore, we hypothesize modeling review content together with review helpfulness is beneficial to review summarization as well.

3 Data

We plan to experiment on three representative review domains: product reviews, book reviews and peer reviews. The first one is mostly studied, while the later two types are more complex, as the review content consists of both reviewer's evaluations of the target and reviewer's references to the target, which is also text. This property makes review summarization more challenging.

For product reviews and book reviews, we plan to use Amazon reviews provided by Jindal and Liu (2008), which is a widely used data set in review mining and sentiment analysis. We consider the helpfulness assessment of an Amazon review as the ratio of "helpful" votes over all votes (Kim et al., 2006). For educational peer reviews, we plan to use an annotated corpus (Nelson and Schunn, 2009) collected from an online peer-review reciprocal system, which we used in our prior work (Xiong and Litman, 2011). Two experts (a writing instructor and a content instructor) were asked to rate the helpfulness of each peer review on a scale from one to five (Pearson correlation r = 0.425, $p \leq 0.01$). For our study, we consider the average ratings given by the two experts (which roughly follow a normal distribution) as the gold standard of review helpfulness ratings. To be consistent with the other review domains, we normalize peer-review helpfulness ratings in the range between 0 and 1.

4 Proposed work

The proposed thesis work consists of three parts: 1) review content analysis using user-provided helpfulness ratings, 2) automatically predicting review helpfulness and 3) a helpfulness-guided review summarization framework.

4.1 Review content analysis

Before advocating the proposed idea, we would test our two hypothesis: 1) user-provided review helpfulness assessment reflects review content difference. 2) Considering review content in terms of **internal content** (e.g. reviewers' opinions) vs. **external content** (e.g. book content), the internal content influences the perceived review helpfulness more than the external content.

We propose to use two kind of instruments, one is Linguistic Inquiry Word Count (LIWC)[1], which is a manually created dictionary of words; the other is the set of review topics learned by Latent Dirichlet Allocation (LDA) (Blei et al., 2003; Blei and McAuliffe, 2010). LIWC analyzes text input based on language usages both syntactically and semantically, which reveals review content patterns at a high level; LDA can be used to model sentence-level review topics which are domain specific.

For the LIWC-based analysis, we test whether each category count has a significant effect on the numerical helpfulness ratings using paired T-test. For LDA-based analysis, we demonstrate the difference by show how the learned topics vary when helpfulness information is introduced as supervision. Specifically, by comparing the topics learned from the unsupervised LDA and those learned from the supervised LDA (with helpfulness ratings), we expect to show that the supervision of helpfulness ratings can yield more meaningful aspect clusters.

It is important to note that in both approaches a review is considered as a bag of words, which might be problematic if the review has both internal and external content. Considering this, we hypothesize that the content difference captured by user-provided helpfulness ratings is mainly in the reviewers' evaluation rather than in the content of external sources (hypothesis 2). We plan to test this hypothesis on both book reviews and peer reviews by analyzing review content in two conditions: in the first condition (the control condition), all content is preserved; in the second condition, the external content is excluded. If we observe more content variance in the second condition than the first one, the second hypothesis is true. Thus we will separate review internal and external content in the later summarization step. For simplification, in the second condition, we only consider the topic words of the external content; we plan to use a corpus-based approach to identify these topic terms and filter them out to reduce the impact of external content.

[1]Url: http://www.liwc.net. We are using LIWC2007.

4.2 Automated review helpfulness assessment

Considering how review usefulness would be integrated in the proposed summarization framework, we propose two models for predicting review helpfulness at different levels of granularity.

A discriminative model to learn review global helpfulness. Previously we (2011) built a discriminative model for predicting the helpfulness of educational peer reviews based on prior work of automatically predicting review helpfulness of product reviews (Kim et al., 2006). We considered both domain-general features and domain-specific features. The domain-general features include structure features (e.g. review length), semantic features, and descriptive statistics of the product ratings (Kim et al., 2006); the domain-specific features include the percentage of external content in reviews and cognitive and social science features that are specific to the peer-review domain. To extend this idea to other types of reviews: for product reviews, we consider product aspect-related terms as the topic words of the external content; for book reviews, we take into account author's profile information (number of books, the mean average book ratings). As we showed that replacing review unigrams with manually crafted keyword categories can further improve the helpfulness model of peer reviews, we plan to investigate whether review unigrams are generally replaceable by review LIWC features for modeling review helpfulness.

A generative model to learn review local helpfulness. In order to utilize user-provided helpfulness information in a decomposable fashion, we propose to use sLDA (Blei and McAuliffe, 2010) to model review content with review helpfulness information at the review level, so that the learned latent topics will be predictive of review helpfulness. In addition to evaluating the model's predictive power and the quality of the learned topics, we will also investigate the extent to which the model's performance is affected by the size of the training set, as we may need to use automatically predicted review helpfulness instead, if user-provided helpfulness information is not available.

4.3 Helpfulness-guided review summarization

In the proposed work, we plan to investigate various methods of supervising an extractive review summarizer using the proposed helpfulness models. The simplest method (M1) is to control review helpfulness of the summarization input by removing reviews that are predicted of low helpfulness. A similar method (M2) is to use post-processing rather than pre-processing – reorder the selected summary candidates (e.g. sentences) based on their predicted helpfulness. The helpfulness of a summary sentence can be either inferred from the local-helpfulness model (sLDA), or aggregated from review-level helpfulness ratings of the review(s) from which the sentence is extracted. The third one (M3) works together with a specific summarization algorithm, interpolating traditional informativeness assessment with novel helpfulness metrics based on the proposed helpfulness models.

For demonstration, we plan to prototype the proposed framework based on MEAD* (Carenini et al., 2006), which is an extension of MEAD (an open-source framework for multi-document summarization (Radev et al., 2004)) for summarizing evaluative text. MEAD* defines sentence informativeness based on features extracted through standard aspect-based review mining (Hu and Liu, 2004). As a human-centric design, we plan to evaluate the proposed framework in a user study in terms of pairwise comparison of the reviews generated by different summarizers (M1, M2, M3 and MEAD*). Although fully automated summarization metrics are available (e.g. Jensen-Shannon Divergence (Louis and Nenkova, 2009)), they favor summaries that have a similar word distribution to the input and thus do not suit our task of review summarization.

To show the generality of the proposed ideas, we plan to evaluate the utility of introducing review helpfulness in aspect ranking as well, which is an important sub-task of review opinion analysis. If our hypothesis (1) is true, we would expect aspect ranking based on helpfulness-involved metrics outperforming the baseline which does not use review helpfulness (Yu et al., 2011). This evaluation will be done on product reviews and peer reviews, as the previous work was based on product reviews, while peer reviews tend to have an objective aspect ranking (provided by domain experts).

5 Contributions

The proposed thesis mainly contributes to review mining and summarization.

1. Investigate the impact of the source of review content on review helpfulness. While a lot of studies focus on product reviews, we based our analysis on a wider range of domains, including peer reviews, which have not been well studied before.

2. Propose two models to automatically assess review helpfulness at different levels of granularity. While the review-level global helpfulness model takes into account domain-specific semantics of helpfulness of reviews, the local helpfulness model learns review helpfulness jointly with review topics. This local helpfulness model allows us to decompose overall review helpfulness into small elements, so that review helpfulness can be easily combined with metrics of other dimensions in assessing the importance of summarization candidates.

3. Propose a user-centric review summarization framework that utilizes user-provided helpfulness assessment as supervision. Compared with previous work, we take a data driven approach in modeling review helpfulness as well as helpfulness-related topics, which requires no extra human input of user-preference and can be adapted to typical review summarization tasks such as aspect selection/ranking, summary sentence ordering, etc.

References

M. Ando and S. Ishizaki. 2012. Analysis of travel review data from readers point of view. *WASSA 2012*, page 47.

D.M. Blei and J.D. McAuliffe. 2010. Supervised topic models. *arXiv preprint arXiv:1003.0783*.

D.M. Blei, A.Y. Ng, and M.I. Jordan. 2003. Latent dirichlet allocation. *the Journal of machine Learning research*, 3:993–1022.

SRK Branavan, H. Chen, J. Eisenstein, and R. Barzilay. 2009. Learning document-level semantic properties from free-text annotations. *Journal of Artificial Intelligence Research*, 34(2):569.

S. Brody and N. Elhadad. 2010. An unsupervised aspect-sentiment model for online reviews. In *Human Language Technologies: The 2010 Annual Conference of the North American Chapter of the Association for Computational Linguistics*, pages 804–812. Association for Computational Linguistics.

G. Carenini, R. Ng, and A. Pauls. 2006. Multi-document summarization of evaluative text. In *In Proceedings of the 11st Conference of the European Chapter of the Association for Computational Linguistics*. Citeseer.

Cristian Danescu-Niculescu-Mizil, Gueorgi Kossinets, Jon Kleinber g, and Lillian Lee. 2009. How opinions are received by online communities: A case study on Amazon .com helpfulness votes. In *Proceedings of WWW*, pages 141–150.

Kavita Ganesan, ChengXiang Zhai, and Jiawei Han. 2010. Opinosis: a graph-based approach to abstractive summarization of highly redundant opinions. In *Proceedings of the 23rd International Conference on Computational Linguistics*, COLING '10, pages 340–348, Stroudsburg, PA, USA. Association for Computational Linguistics.

Anindya Ghose and Panagiotis G. Ipeirotis. 2008. Estimating the socio-economic impact of product reviews. In *NYU Stern Research Working Paper CeDER*.

M. Hu and B. Liu. 2004. Mining and summarizing customer reviews. In *Proceedings of the tenth ACM SIGKDD international conference on Knowledge discovery and data mining*, pages 168–177. ACM.

N. Jindal and B. Liu. 2008. Opinion spam and analysis. In *Proceedings of the international conference on Web search and web data mining*, pages 219–230.

H.D. Kim and C.X. Zhai. 2009. Generating comparative summaries of contradictory opinions in text. In *Proceedings of the 18th ACM conference on Information and knowledge management*, pages 385–394. ACM.

Soo-Min Kim, Patrick Pantel, Tim Chklovski, and Marco Pennacchiotti. 2006. Automatically assessing review helpfulness. In *Proceedings of the 2006 Conference on Empirical Methods in Natural Language Processing (EMNLP2006)*, pages 423–430, Sydney, Australia, July.

K. Lerman, S. Blair-Goldensohn, and R. McDonald. 2009. Sentiment summarization: Evaluating and learning user preferences. In *Proceedings of the 12th Conference of the European Chapter of the Association for Computational Linguistics*, pages 514–522. Association for Computational Linguistics.

Annie Louis and Ani Nenkova. 2009. Automatically evaluating content selection in summarization without human models. In *Proceedings of the 2009 Conference on Empirical Methods in Natural Language Processing: Volume 1-Volume 1*, pages 306–314. Association for Computational Linguistics.

Y. Lu and C. Zhai. 2008. Opinion integration through semi-supervised topic modeling. In *Proceedings of the 17th international conference on World Wide Web*, pages 121–130. ACM.

Q. Mei, X. Ling, M. Wondra, H. Su, and C.X. Zhai. 2007. Topic sentiment mixture: modeling facets and opinions in weblogs. In *Proceedings of the 16th international conference on World Wide Web*, pages 171–180. ACM.

S.M. Mudambi and D. Schuff. 2010. What makes a helpful online review? a study of customer reviews on amazon. com. *MIS quarterly*, 34(1):185–200.

A. Mukherjee and B. Liu. 2012. aspect extraction through semi-supervised modeling. In *Proceedings of 50th anunal meeting of association for computational Linguistics (acL-2012)(accepted for publication)*.

Melissa M. Nelson and Christian D. Schunn. 2009. The nature of feedback: how different types of peer feedback affect writing performance. In *Instructional Science*, volume 37, pages 375–401.

A.M. Popescu and O. Etzioni. 2005. Extracting product features and opinions from reviews. In *Proceedings of the conference on Human Language Technology and Empirical Methods in Natural Language Processing*, pages 339–346. Association for Computational Linguistics.

D. Radev, T. Allison, S. Blair-Goldensohn, J. Blitzer, A. Celebi, S. Dimitrov, E. Drabek, A. Hakim, W. Lam, D. Liu, et al. 2004. Mead-a platform for multidocument multilingual text summarization. In *Proceedings of LREC*, volume 2004.

C. Sauper and R. Barzilay. 2013. Automatic aggregation by joint modeling of aspects and values. *Journal of Artificial Intelligence Research*, 46:89–127.

V. Stoyanov and C. Cardie. 2008. Topic identification for fine-grained opinion analysis. In *Proceedings of the 22nd International Conference on Computational Linguistics-Volume 1*, pages 817–824. Association for Computational Linguistics.

I. Titov and R. McDonald. 2008a. A joint model of text and aspect ratings for sentiment summarization. *Urbana*, 51:61801.

I. Titov and R. McDonald. 2008b. Modeling online reviews with multi-grain topic models. In *Proceedings of the 17th international conference on World Wide Web*, pages 111–120. ACM.

Wenting Xiong and Diane Litman. 2011. Automatically predicting peer-review helpfulness. In *Proceedings of the 49th Annual Meeting of the Association for Computational Linguistics: Human Language Technologies*, pages 502–507.

J. Yu, Z.J. Zha, M. Wang, and T.S. Chua. 2011. Aspect ranking: identifying important product aspects from online consumer reviews. *Computational Linguistics*, pages 1496–1505.

Entrainment in Spoken Dialogue Systems: Adopting, Predicting and Influencing User Behavior

Rivka Levitan
Department of Computer Science
Columbia University
New York, NY 10027, USA
rlevitan@cs.columbia.edu

Abstract

Entrainment is the phenomenon of the speech of conversational partners becoming more similar to each other. This thesis proposal presents a comprehensive look at entrainment in human conversations and how entrainment may be incorporated into the design of spoken dialogue systems in order to improve system performance and user satisfaction. We compare different kinds of entrainment in both classic and novel dimensions, provide experimental results on the utility of entrainment, and show that entrainment can be used to improve a system's ASR performance and turn-taking decisions.

1 Introduction

Entrainment is the phenomenon of interlocutors becoming more similar to each other in their speech in the course of a conversation. Entrainment has been observed in numerous domains and for multiple levels of communication. In addition, many studies have shown associations between entrainment and desirable dialogue characteristics. The proposed work aims to improve spoken dialogue system performance both qualitatively and quantitatively by exploiting this prevalent and significant phenomenon. Spoken dialogue systems can significantly improve the quality of their user interactions by incorporating entrainment into their design:

- A spoken dialogue system can entrain to its users, adjusting its own output to align with theirs. This should improve the dialogue quality as perceived by the user.
- It can exploit the concept of entrainment by changing the parameters of its own output when it wants the user to speak differently. For example, when the user is speaking too quickly, the system can slow down its own output, causing the user to do the same.
- It can use an entrainment model along with information about its own behavior to more accurately predict how the user will behave.

Our proposed work explores the role of entrainment in human conversations and looks at how it can improve interactions with spoken dialogue systems. In addition to presenting an in-depth study of the characteristics of human entrainment, we will demonstrate that spoken dialogue systems can use this information to predict characteristics of the user's speech, improve the user's impression of the dialogue quality and system persona by adopting the user's speech characteristics, and improve recognition accuracy by influencing the user to abandon prosodic characteristics associated with ASR error.

This thesis proposal is organized as follows: Section 2 discusses the literature related to the proposed work. Section 3 describes the corpus used in these studies. Section 4 addresses the question of how humans entrain and how this information can be used to more accurately predict a user's behavior. Section 5 discusses how entrainment affects the perceived quality of human and human-computer conversations, and Section 6 explores how entrainment can be used to influence user behavior. Section 7 describes the main contributions of this work.

Proceedings of the NAACL HLT 2013 Student Research Workshop, pages 84–90,
Atlanta, Georgia, 13 June 2013.

2 Related work

Entrainment has been shown to occur at almost every level of human communication: lexical (Brennan and Clark, 1992), syntactic (Reitter and Moore, 2007; Ward and Litman, 2007), stylistic (Niederhoffer and Pennebaker, 2002; Danescu-Niculescu-Mizil et al., 2011), acoustic-prosodic (Natale, 1975; Coulston et al., 2002; Ward and Litman, 2007) and phonetic (Pardo, 2006).

Entrainment in many of these dimensions has also been associated with measures of dialogue success. Chartrand and Bargh (1999), for example, demonstrated that subjects who interacted with confederates who mimicked their posture and behavior reported greater liking for the confederate and a smoother interaction. Lee et al. (2010) found that entrainment measures derived from pitch features were significantly higher in positive interactions between married couples in therapy than in negative interactions. Looking at more objective measures, Nenkova et al. (2008) found that the degree of entrainment on high-frequency words was correlated with task score and turn-taking features.

These studies have been motivated by theoretical models such as Giles' Communication Accommodation Theory (Giles et al., 1987), which proposes that speakers promote social approval or efficient communication by adapting to their interlocutors' communicative behavior. Another theory informing the association of entrainment and dialogue success is the coordination-rapport hypothesis (Tickle-Degnen and Rosenthal, 1990), which posits that the degree of liking between conversational partners should be correlated with the degree of nonverbal coordination between them. In contrast, Chartrand and Bargh (1999) posit that entrainment is a purely automatic process, a product of the perception-behavior link, which predicts that the act of observing a behavior makes the observer more likely to engage in that behavior as well.

3 Columbia Games Corpus

Many of the studies in this work were conducted on the Columbia Games Corpus (Gravano, 2009), a collection of twelve dyadic conversations elicited from native speakers of Standard American English. During the collection of the corpus, each pair of participants played a set of computer games that required them to verbally cooperate to achieve a mutual goal. In the Cards games, one speaker described the cards she saw on her screen, and her partner attempted to match them to the cards on his own screen. In the Objects games, one speaker described the location of an object on her screen, and her partner attempted to place the corresponding object in exactly the same location on his own screen. For both games, the participants received points based on how exact a match was; they later were paid for each point.

The corpus consists of approximately nine hours of recorded dialogue. It has been orthographically transcribed and annotated with prosodic and turn-taking labels. Thirteen subjects participated in the collection of the corpus, and nine returned on another day for a second session with a different partner. This is useful for our study of entrainment, since we can compare a single speaker's behavior with two different interlocutors. In addition, the corpus is representative of the kind of speech we are interested in: task-oriented dialogue between strangers.

4 Entrainment in human conversations

We begin our study of entrainment by looking at entrainment in human conversations. Aside from the interest inherent in advancing our understanding of this human behavior, research in this area can inform the design of spoken dialogue systems. A system that entrains the way a human does will seem more natural, and a system that knows how humans entrain can use this information to better predict how a user will behave, improving its own performance.

4.1 Acoustic-prosodic entrainment

This study, previously presented in (Levitan and Hirschberg, 2011), creates a cohesive view of entrainment by directly comparing entrainment on a set of acoustic-prosodic features, measured in five different ways. By comparing these different measures of entrainment, we bring clarity to three aspects of entrainment:

- *Is it global or local?* Two speakers may fluctuate around similar means, while diverging widely at any specific point. Conversely, they may be globally dissimilar, but locally they may be relatively similar.
- *Is it by value or by direction?* If a speaker en-

trains to her partner's actual value, if he lowers his voice, she may raise her own in order to match his new intensity. If she matches the direction of the change rather than the new value, she will lower her voice as well, even if this results in a value less similar to his.

- *Is the degree of entrainment static, or does it improve?* Do speakers converge—become more similar—as the conversation progresses?

The features we examine are intensity mean and max, pitch mean and max, jitter, shimmer, noise-to-harmonics ratio (NHR), and syllables per second[1]. We look for evidence of *global* entrainment by comparing the similarities in feature means between partners with the similarities between speakers who are not conversational partners.

We see an effect of entrainment for almost all the features. In addition, the difference between partners for several of the features is smaller in the second half of the conversation, constituting evidence of *convergence*. We also find a strong effect of *local* entrainment: for every feature, adjacent turns are significantly ($p < 0.001$) more similar to each other than non-adjacent turns. We conclude that entrainment is by value rather than by direction; that global entrainment exists in addition to local matching for several features, most notably intensity; and that entrainment is dynamic for some features, improving as the conversation progresses.

4.2 Entrainment on outliers

Since entrainment is generally considered an unconscious phenomenon, it is interesting to consider entrainment when a feature is particularly salient. The theory that the perception-behavior link is the mechanism behind entrainment (Chartrand and Bargh, 1999) would predict that the effect of entrainment would be stronger in this case, since such features are more likely to be observed and therefore imitated. We test this hypothesis by looking at cases in which one speaker in a pair has a feature value in the 90th or 10th percentile. This study was previously described in (Levitan et al., 2012).

As in our tests for global entrainment (Section 4.1), we compute a partner and non-partner similarity for each speaker. The partner similarity should be lower for outlier pairs (pairs in which one speaker has an outlier feature value), and the non-partner similarity should be lower as well, since the outlier speaker diverges from the norm. We therefore can expect the difference between these two values to be the same for outlier and typical pairs. If this difference is lower for outlier pairs, we can conclude that the effect of entrainment is weaker in outlier cases. We find, in fact, that this difference is *greater* for outlier pairs for several features, indicating that speakers entrain *more* to outlier values of these features. This finding supports the perception-behavior link. In addition, it has implications for cases in which it is an objective to induce one's interlocutor to entrain, as we will discuss in Section 6.

4.3 Entrainment and backchannel-inviting cues

Backchannels are short, nondisruptive segments of speech that a speaker utters to let his interlocutor know that he is keeping up. They are extremely prevalent in task-oriented conversation. Gravano and Hirschberg (2009) identified six acoustic and prosodic features that tend to be different before backchannels, hypothesizing that these features serve as cues to one's interlocutor that a backchannel would be welcome. Individual speakers use different sets of cues, and can differ in their realization of a cue. We look for evidence of entrainment on backchannel-inviting cues. This work, previously discussed in (Levitan et al., 2011), represents a first look at entrainment in a pragmatic dimension.

We measure backchannel-inviting cues in three ways. Firstly, we measure the similarity of the speaker pairs' cue sets by counting the number of cues they have in common, and find that partners have more cues in common than non-partners. Secondly, we measure the similarity of cue realization, and show that feature values before backchannels for pitch, intensity and voice quality are more similar between partners. In addition, this measure shows evidence of convergence for pitch and intensity, which are more similar before backchannels in the second half of a conversation. Finally, we measure the local effect of this entrainment by correlating feature values before consecutive backchannels

[1]Intensity mean is an acoustic measure perceived as loudness, and intensity max represents the range of loudness. Jitter, shimmer and NHR are three measures of voice quality; jitter and shimmer are perceived as harshness, and NHR as hoarseness. Syllables per second measure speaking rate.

and find that pitch and intensity before backchannels are moderately correlated.

4.4 Future work

We have shown that a speaker's conversational behavior is influenced by that of her interlocutor. We therefore propose to develop a framework for using entrainment information to label or predict a speaker's behavior. An example of such a task is predicting backchannels. Based on the work of Gravano and Hirschberg (2009), a system deciding whether to produce a backchannel or take the floor should compare the user's most recent utterance to a backchannel-preceding model and a turn-yielding model. Since each speaker uses a different count of backchannel-preceding cues, a model trained on other speakers may not be useful. However, data from the user may not be available and is likely to be sparse at best.

Since interlocutors use similar backchannel-inviting cues, we can use information from the interlouctor – the system – to build the model. The influence of this interlocutor information can be weighted according to the probable strength of the entrainment effect, which can depend, as we have shown, on the feature being predicted, the respective genders of the participants, whether a feature value is an outlier, and where in the conversation the speech segment occurs.

5 Entrainment and dialogue quality

This section addresses two main research questions:

1. What kinds of entrainment are most important to conversational quality?
2. Will the passive benefits of entrainment apply when it is a computer that is entraining?

To answer the first question, we look at the entrainment correlates of social and objective variables in the Games Corpus (previously reported in Levitan et al., 2012). We address the second question with a Wizard of Oz study that looks at subjects' reactions to an entraining spoken dialogue system.

5.1 Entrainment correlates of dialogue characteristics

Lexical entrainment has been associated with measures of smooth turn-taking and task success (Nenkova et al., 2008). Here, we correlate entrainment on intensity mean and max, pitch mean and max, jitter, shimmer, noise-to-harmonics ratio (NHR), and syllables per second with four objective measures of dialogue coordination: number of turns, mean turn latency, percentage of overlaps, and percentage of interruptions. We interpret a high number of turns and percentage of overlaps (cases in which one person begins speaking as her interlocutor finishes his turn) as signs of a smoothly flowing, well-coordinated conversation. We therefore expect them to be positively associated with entrainment, in line with previous work and the theory that entrainment facilitates communication. In contrast, high turn latency (the lag time between turns) and percentage of interruptions (cases in which one person begins speaking before her interlocutor has finished his turn) are signs of poor turn-taking behavior and an awkward conversation. We therefore expect them to be negatively correlated with entrainment measures.

To look at more perceptual measures of dialogue quality, we used Amazon Mechanical Turk[2] to annotate each task (the sub-units of each game) in the Games Corpus for what we term *social variables*, the perceived social characteristics of an interaction and ints participants. Details on the annotation process can be found in (Gravano et al., 2011). In this study, we focus on four social variables: *trying to be liked*, *giving encouragement*, *trying to dominate*, and *conversation awkward*. Based on Communication Accommodation Theory (Giles et al., 1987), we expect the first two social variables, which represent the desire to minimize social distance, to be positively correlated with entrainment. Someone who is *trying to dominate*, on the other hand, will try to increase social distance, and we therefore expect this variable to correlate negatively with entrainment, as should *conversation awkward*.

We report separate results for female, male and mixed-gender pairs. In general, we see correlations in the expected directions: the number of turns, percentage of overlaps, and *giving encouragement* are positively correlated with entrainment for all gender groups, latency is negatively correlated with entrainment for male and female pairs, and *trying to be liked* is positively correlated with entrainment for

[2]http://www.mturk.com

male and mixed-gender pairs. We see no correlations for *trying to dominate*, possibly because annotators were confused between the socially weak position of *trying* to dominate, and the socially powerful position of actually dominating.

For objective variables, we see the strongest and most numerous correlations for male pairs, while for objective variables, this is true for mixed-gender pairs, leading us to conclude that entrainment is most important to the coordination of a conversation for male pairs and to the perceived quality of a conversation for mixed-gender pairs. We identify intensity as an important entrainment feature, as well as shimmer for dialogue coordination for female or mixed-gender pairs. In future work, we plan to correlate these social and objective variables with measures of local entrainment and convergence (Section 4.1).

5.2 Entrainment and dialogue quality in spoken dialogue systems

In this study (currently ongoing), we look at whether subjects will attribute more positive qualities to an interaction with a system whose voice is more similar to their own. To answer this question, we create a Wizard of Oz setup in which a subject interacts with an *entrained* voice and a *disentrained* voice. We chose to employ a wizard instead of a fully functional dialogue system in order to neutralize possible intrusions from other components of a dialogue system and isolate the entrainment effect.

The subjects are given three tasks modeled on reasons for which someone might call 311, New York City's phone number for government information. In the *taxi* scenario, for example, the subject is given a description of an incident in which a taxi drove unsafely, and is told to report the incident to the system, using the given date, time and location. Using this paradigm, we can collect spontaneous speech while still being able to use prerecorded prompts: the content is predetermined, but the sentence form and word choice is up to the subject.

For the first task, *alternate side parking*, the experimenter prints prompts to the subject's screen using a chat program, and the subject responds by speaking into a headset that plays into the experimenter's computer. The purpose of this first task is to get a sample of the subject's speech. The subject then fills out some demographic forms and the NEO-FFI personality test, while the experimenter calculates the vocal intensity and speaking rate of the subject's speech. A set of prerecorded prompts is then scaled to match the subject's vocal parameters, forming an *entrained* set, and then scaled away from the subject's parameters, forming the *disentrained* set. The parameters for the disentrained set were chosen empirically to result in a voice perceptibly different from the entrained set while remaining undistorted and natural-sounding.

The subject then completes two more tasks, one with the *entrained* voice and one with the *disentrained* voice. We vary the order and combination of tasks and voices so we can test for effects of order and task. After each task, the subject fills out a survey containing questions like "I liked the system's personality" or "I found talking with the system annoying." We hypothesize that they will agree more with positive statements about the entraining version of the system.

We also crudely measure each subject's perceptual sensitivity to vocal characteristics by asking them to describe each voice by choosing from a list of adjectives like "high-pitched," "fast," or "loud." We will look at how this sensitivity, as well as gender and personality, interact with the subjects' reactions to the system's entrainment.

6 Influencing user behavior

In human conversations, it is common for a speaker to attempt to affect his interlocutor's behavior by modeling a desired change. For example, a speaker may raise his own voice if he is having trouble hearing and wishes his interlocutor to speak more loudly. Since humans have been shown to entrain to computers (Coulston et al., 2002; Stoyanchev and Stent, 2009; Bell et al., 2003), it is reasonable for a spoken dialogue system to use this strategy to influence its user to speak in a way that will optimize the performance of its automatic speech recognition (ASR). A previous study (Lopes et al., 2011) successfully induced users to abandon words prone to ASR error simply by removing those words from the system's prompts. In this work, we attempt to influence users to abandon prosodic characteristics associated with ASR failure by modeling the desired change in the system's prompts.

Hirschberg et al. (2004) found that utterances that followed longer pauses or were louder, longer, or pitched higher were less likely to be recognized correctly. Our method looks for these undesirable prosodic features in utterances with low ASR confidence and attempts to induce the user to abandon them. We hypothesize that abandoning prosody associated with ASR failure will result in improved ASR performance.

Our approach is as follows. When the system's ASR returns a hypothesis with low confidence for an utterance, it finds the utterance's intensity, pitch and duration. If any of these features fall within the range of utterances that tend to be misrecognized, the system employs one of four strategies. The **explicit** strategy is to ask the user to make the desired change, e.g. "Please speak more quietly." The **entrainment** strategy is to model the desired change, e.g. lowering the intensity of the system's output. The **explicit+entrainment** strategy combines the two, e.g. by saying "Please speak more quietly" in a quieter system voice. We hypothesize that one strategy may increase the efficacy of the other. We will also try a **no strategy** condition as a baseline for how often the user independently abandons the undesirable prosody.

Each strategy will be embodied in a simple request for repetition. For each strategy, we will look at how often the subsequent turn displays the desired change in prosody. In addition, we will see how often the ASR performance improves on the subsequent turn. A third measure of a strategy's success will be the durability of its effect—that is, how likely the undesirable prosody is to recur later in the conversation.

Within the entrainment condition, we will test how pronounced a change must be in order to induce a corresponding change on the part of the user. Our research on outlier entrainment suggests that a more extreme change is more likely to be entrained to. However, the most attractive feature of the entrainment condition is its nondisruptiveness, and this quality will be lost if the change in the system's voice is too extreme. We will therefore begin with a slight change, and test how much the degree of change must be increased before the user will imitate it.

Fandrianto and Eskenazi (2012) implemented a similar approach, lowering the system's vocal intensity or increasing its speaking rate when its classifiers detected the speaking styles of shouting or hyperarticulation. By responding to individual prosodic features instead of higher-level speaking styles, we avoid the layer of error introduced by classifiers. Furthermore, our approach can account for cases in which ASR error is caused by prosodic features that do not comprise an identifiable speaking style. Finally, our detailed analysis will give more information about the advantages and limitations of each strategy.

7 Contributions

The studies of human-human conversations in this thesis will advance current understanding of how people entrain. We provide a cohesive picture of entrainment by directly comparing different measures on a single corpus, establishing that entrainment is both a global and a local phenomenon, that people entrain by value rather than by direction, and that it is a dynamic process, improving with the course of a dialogue. We show that speaker pairs entrain in a novel dimension, backchannel-inviting cues, and that this entrainment is associated with task success and dialogue coordination. We also show that the effect of entrainment is stronger in outlier cases, lending experimental support to the perception-behavior link.

This work provides experimental results on the utility of entrainment in conversations with both humans and spoken dialogue systems. In human conversations, we show that entrainment is correlated with positive social characteristics and turn-taking features. In our Wizard of Oz experiments, we will show how entrainment affects a user's perception of the quality of a spoken dialogue system.

Finally, this work shows how the principles of entrainment can be used to actively improve spoken dialogue systems. We will build a framework for implementing the results of our studies of entrainment in human conversations into prediction models, which we hypothesize will improve their accuracy and can be used to improve a system's performance. In our influencing experiments, we will attempt to influence a user to speak in a way that will optimize ASR performance simply by changing the system's own voice.

References

Linda Bell, Joakim Gustafson, and Mattias Heldner. Prosodic adaptation in human-computer interaction. In *Proceedings of ICPHS'03*, pages 833–836, 2003.

Susan E. Brennan and Herbert H. Clark. Conceptual pacts and lexical choice in conversation. *Journal of Experimental Psychology: Learning, Memory and Cognition*, 22(6): 1482–1493, 1992.

T. L. Chartrand and J. A. Bargh. The chameleon effect: The perception-behavior link and social interaction. *Journal of Personality and Social Psychology*, 76(6):893–910, 1999.

Rachel Coulston, Sharon Oviatt, and Courtney Darves. Amplitude convergence in children's conversational speech with animated personas. In *Proceedings of ICSLP'02*, 2002.

Cristian Danescu-Niculescu-Mizil, Michael Gamon, and Susan Dumais. Mark my words! linguistic style accommodation in social media. In *Proceedings of WWW*, 2011.

Andrew Fandrianto and Maxine Eskenazi. Prosodic entrainment in an information-driven dialog system. In *Proceedings of Interspeech*, 2012.

H. Giles, A. Mulac, J.J. Bradac, and P. Johnson. *Speech accommodation theory: the first decade and beyond*. Sage, Beverly Hills, CA, 1987.

Agustín Gravano. *Turn-taking and affirmative cue words in task-oriented dialogue*. PhD thesis, Columbia University, 2009.

Agustín Gravano and Julia Hirschberg. Backchannel-inviting cues in task-oriented dialogue. In *Proceedings of Interspeech*, 2009.

Agustín Gravano, Rivka Levitan, Laura Willson, Stefan Benus, Julia Hirschberg, and Ani Nenkova. Acoustic and prosodic correlates of social behavior. In *Proceedings of Interspeech*, 2011.

Julia Hirschberg, Diane Litman, and Marc Swerts. Prosodic and other cues to speech recognition failures. *Speech Communication*, 43:155–175, 2004.

Chi-Chun Lee, Matthew Black, Athanasios Katsamanis, Adam Lammert, Brian Baucom, Andrew Christensen, Panayiotis G. Georgiou, and Shrikanth Narayanan. Quantification of prosodic entrainment in affective spontaneous spoken interactions of married couples. In *Proceedings of Interspeech*, 2010.

Rivka Levitan and Julia Hirschberg. Measuring acoustic-prosodic entrainment with respect to multiple levels and dimensions. In *Proceedings of Interspeech*, 2011.

Rivka Levitan, Agustín Gravano, and Julia Hirschberg. Entrainment in speech preceding backchannels. In *Proceedings of the 49th Annual Meeting of the Association for Computational Linguistics*, 2011.

Rivka Levitan, Agustín Gravano, Laura Willson, Stefan Benus, Julia Hirschberg, and Ani Nenkova. Acoustic-prosodic entrainment and social behavior. In *Proceedings of the 2012 Conference of the North American Chapter of the Association for Computational Linguistics: Human Language Technologies*, pages 11–19, Montréal, Canada, June 2012. Association for Computational Linguistics. URL `http://www.aclweb.org/anthology/N12-1002`.

José Lopes, Maxine Eskenazi, and Isabel Trancoso. Towards choosing better primes for spoken dialog systems. In *ASRU'11*, pages 306–311, 2011.

Michael Natale. Convergence of mean vocal intensity in dyadic communication as a function of social desirability. *Journal of Personality and Social Psychology*, 32(5):790–804, 1975.

Ani Nenkova, Agustín Gravano, and Julia Hirschberg. High frequency word entrainment in spoken dialogue. In *Proceedings of ACL/HLT*, 2008.

Kate G. Niederhoffer and James W. Pennebaker. Linguistic style matching in social interaction. *Journal of Language and Social Psychology*, 21(4):337–360, 2002.

Jennifer S. Pardo. On phonetic convergence during conversational interaction. *Journal of the Acoustic Society of America*, 19(4), 2006.

David Reitter and Johanna D. Moore. Predicting success in dialogue. In *Proceedings of the 45th Annual Meeting of the Association of Computational Linguistics*, pages 808–815, 2007.

Svetlana Stoyanchev and Amanda Stent. Lexical and syntactic priming and their impact in deployed spoken dialog systems. In *Proceedings of NAACL HLT*, 2009.

Linda Tickle-Degnen and Robert Rosenthal. The nature of rapport and its nonverbal correlates. *Psychological Inquiry*, 1 (4):285–293, 1990.

Arthur Ward and Diane Litman. Measuring convergence and priming in tutorial dialog. Technical report, University of Pittsburgh, 2007.

User Goal Change Model for Spoken Dialog State Tracking

Yi Ma
Department of Computer Science & Engineering
The Ohio State University
Columbus, OH 43210, USA
may@cse.ohio-state.edu

Abstract

In this paper, a Maximum Entropy Markov Model (MEMM) for dialog state tracking is proposed to efficiently handle user goal evolvement in two steps. The system first predicts the occurrence of a user goal change based on linguistic features and dialog context for each dialog turn, and then the proposed model could utilize this user goal change information to infer the most probable dialog state sequence which underlies the evolvement of user goal during the dialog. It is believed that with the suggested various domain independent feature functions, the proposed model could better exploit not only the intra-dependencies within long ASR N-best lists but also the inter-dependencies of the observations across dialog turns, which leads to more efficient and accurate dialog state inference.

1 Introduction

The ability to converse with humans is usually considered the most important characteristic which defines the intelligent nature of a machine. In recent years, advanced approaches for handling different components within a spoken dialogue system have been proposed and studied. Both statistical inference methods for dialog state tracking and machine learning techniques (such as reinforcement learning) for automatic policy optimization are active domains of research, which implies that there are still many open challenges in this field that are worth being explored. One of such challenges is how to better exploit the ASR (Automatic Speech Recognition) N-best list when the top ASR hypothesis is incorrect. Furthermore, reasoning over different ASR N-best lists is also difficult since it is hard to decide when to detect commonality (when user repeats) and when to look for differences (when user changes her or his mind) among multiple ASR N-best lists. Another challenge is how to handle more complex user actions such as negotiating alternative choices or seeking out other potential solutions when interacting with the system.

This proposal presents a probabilistic framework for modeling the evolvement of user goal during the dialog (focusing on the shaded component *Dialog State Tracking* in Figure 1 that shows a typical diagram for a spoken dialog system), which aims to endow the system with the ability to model natural negotiation strategies, in the hope of leading to more accurate and efficient dialog state tracking performance.

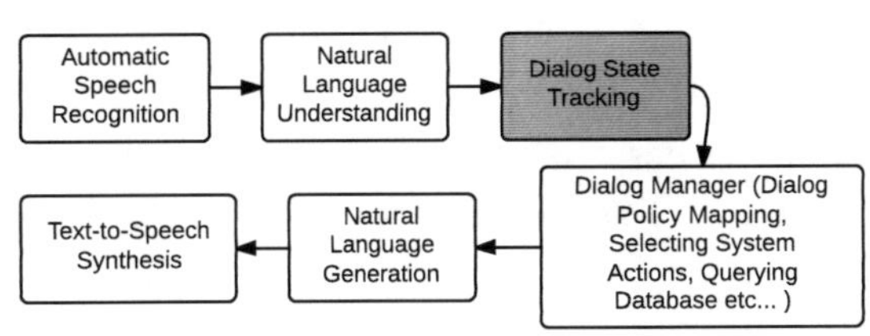

Figure 1: a typical spoken dialogue system

2 Unanswered Challenges for Spoken Dialog Systems

Due to the inevitable erroneous hypotheses made by the speech recognizer as well as the ubiquitous ambiguity existing in the natural language understand-

Proceedings of the NAACL HLT 2013 Student Research Workshop, pages 91–97,
Atlanta, Georgia, 13 June 2013. ©2013 Association for Computational Linguistics

ing process, it is impossible for a spoken dialog system to observe the true user goal directly. Therefore, methods to efficiently infer the true hidden dialog states from noisy observations over multiple dialog turns become crucial for building a robust spoken dialog system.

The POMDP (Partially Observable Markov Decision Process) framework has been proposed to maintain multiple dialog state hypotheses under uncertainty with automated dialog policy learning (Williams and Young, 2007; Henderson et al., 2008; Thomson and Young, 2010; Young et al., 2010). Although the original POMDP framework suffers difficulties of scaling up the model to handle real-world domains in practice, it provides a unified statistical framework for existing techniques with global optimization. Partition-based approaches (Gašić and Young, 2011; Williams, 2010; Young et al., 2010) attempt to group user goals into a number of partitions and won't split a partition unless when a distinction is required by observations. Due to this property, partition-based methods could have high scalability for more complex practical domains.

Bayesian network based approximate methods also emerged to tackle the complexity of representing and tracking multiple dialog states within probabilistic frameworks (Raux and Ma, 2011; Thomson and Young, 2010). In previous work, we presented a new probabilistic model – DPOT (Dynamic Probabilistic Ontology Trees) – to track dialog state in a spoken dialog system (Raux and Ma, 2011). DPOT captures both the user goal and the history of user dialog acts (user actions) using a unified Bayesian network. Efficient inference (a form of blocked Gibbs sampling) is performed to exploit the structure of the model. Evaluation on a corpus of dialogs from the CMU Let's Go system shows that DPOT significantly outperforms a deterministic baseline by exploiting long ASR N-best lists without loss of accuracy. At any point in the dialog, the joint distribution over the goal network represents the inferred dialog state about the user goal.[1] The goal network of DPOT does not expand per time slice for each turn but the evidence accumulates as the dialog progresses. Therefore the model becomes inefficient when users change their mind – user has to repeat multiple times in order to possibly trigger a goal change in the inferred dialog state.

System: How can I help you?
User: I would like a flight from Columbus to San Francisco.
System: I hear you say you want a flight from Columbus to San Francisco, is that correct?
User: Yes.
System: OK, at what time?
User: Saturday morning.
System: Leaving on Saturday morning. Searching available flights... [some time later] I have found one flight from CMH to SFO leaving at 7am on Saturday morning. Do you want me to print out itinerary, make flight reservation or hear more information about the flight?
User: How about Sunday morning?
System: Sorry I am afraid I didn't catch that. You can say print itinerary, book flight or more information.
User: None of them. Do you have any flights leaving on Sunday morning instead?
System: Sorry, what can I do for you? [system reset itself for a new dialog to recover from the failure]
User: ...

Figure 2: Example of user goal change: at the end of the dialog the user would like to explore alternative flights at a different time, but the dialog system did not expect such a user action, leading to a system failure

Current approaches often assume that user would have a fixed goal in his or her mind before conversing with the system and this single goal remains unchanged throughout the dialog. However, the key question we would like to raise here is that whether the assumption that a user would not change her or his mind during the dialog is reasonable or not in the first place.[2] Figure 2 shows an example where user goal evolves as the dialog moves on. In this example, the system did not catch the partial change of user goal and failed to return alternative answers given a new request from the user – now the fixed goal assumption has been challenged. Moreover, sometimes people do not even have a clear goal in their minds before they start speaking to the system (e.g., a user might want a flight from Columbus to San Francisco during the coming weekend, but the exact departure date depends on user's schedule as well as the price of the ticket.). From the example dialog shown in Figure 2, clearly it can be noticed that there are some useful hints or linguistic patterns – such as *How about ...?* and ... *instead?* – which could be extracted from the user's spoken language

[1]In the Let's Go bus information system, a user goal is decomposed into three concepts: `Bus` (the bus number), `Orig` (the origin stop) and `Dest` (the destination stop).

[2]It is true that for some simple domains such as luggage retrieval or call routing, users are less likely to change their mind.

as predictors for potential user goal change. We can then further use this predicted information (user goal changed or not) to better infer the true user goal and prevent a system failure or start over. In fact, it is this intuition that forms the basis of the proposed methods.

However, existing methods heavily rely on the assumption that user won't change her or his mind throughout the dialog. In order to keep the computations tractable in practice, POMDP-based methods often assume that user goal does not change during the dialog (Young et al., 2010). Moreover, within the POMDP framework there is a user action model which would suppress the weights of conflict observations for those slots which have already been filled – the intuition is that if a value for a certain slot has already been provided or observed, it is less likely that a new value will be provided again (based on the assumption of fixed user goal) and it is more likely to be a speech recognition error instead (Williams and Young, 2007). Furthermore, one of the claimed benefit for existing statistical dialog state inference methods is the ability to exploit the information lower down from ASR N-best lists by aggregating weak information across multiple dialog turns – the intuition is that overlapped consistent weak evidence is sometimes a useful hint for predicting the underlying true user goal (as illustrated in Figure 3) – again it implies that the user would repeatedly refine the same goal until the machine gets it.

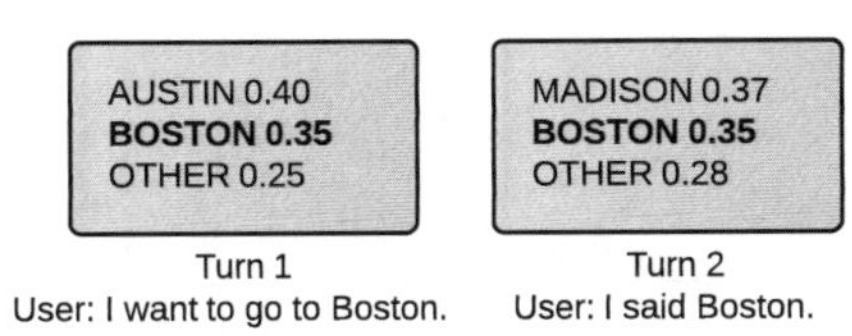

Figure 3: Given the fact that user action BOSTON has been repeatedly observed as DEPARTURE_CITY across the first two turns – although not at the top position of the ASR N-best list – existing statistical dialog state tracking algorithms would capture this pattern and put a strong bias on BOSTON as the inferred user goal.

It is true that putting such a constraint – assuming a fixed user goal during the dialog – simplifies the computational complexity, it also sacrifices the flexibility and usability of a spoken dialog system. Although one could think of some hand-crafted and ad-hoc rules such as explicit or implicit confirmation/disconfirmation to deal with sudden user goal changes during a dialog, it increases the number of dialog turns and makes the dialog system less natural and user friendly.

3 Spoken Dialog State Tracking with Explicit Model of User Goal Change

3.1 *BuildByVoice* Domain

In fact, there are many situations where frequent user goal changes would be highly expected (i.e. the user might try to *negotiate* with the system). These domains might include but not limited to finding nearby restaurants or hotels, searching for movies to watch, ordering food or online shopping, etc., in which users are very likely to explore different alternatives and their goals would probably change frequently as the dialog progresses.

Figure 4: An experimental web interface prototype for *BuildByVoice* – a spoken dialog system aimed to assist potential car buyers to customize a car by voice

Considering one typical example among those domains – a spoken interactive system which could allow a user to configure a new car by speech (a prototype web interface of the *BuildByVoice* system is shown in Figure 4[3]) – one could imagine the user would tend to experiment many possible combinations of different configurations for a car. Indeed that is the purpose of having such a system so that users could preview the resulting effect before a real car is made. A *BuildByVoice* domain may consist of

[3]A baseline *BuildByVoice* system by using DPOT for dialog state tracking (without user goal change detection) is under implementation. The baseline system will be deployed to Amazon Mechanical Turk for initial data collection.

the following five independent concepts with their possible values listed as follows:[4]

Model: `Accord Coupe`, `Accord Sedan`, `Accord Plug-In`, `Civic Coupe`, `Civic Sedan,...`[5]

Engine: `V4`, `V4 Turbo`, `V4 Sport`, `V6`, `V6 Turbo`, `V6 Sport,...`

Exterior Color: `Toffee Brown`, `Coffee Brown`, `Candy Brown`, `Night Blue`, `Moonlight Blue`, `Midnight Blue,...`

Interior Color: `Black Leather`, `Black Vinyl`, `Gray Leather`, `Gray Vinyl`, `Brown Leather`, `Brown Vinyl,...`

Wheels: `17 inches Steel`, `17 inches Alloy`, `18 inches Steel`, `18 inches Alloy`, `18 inches Polished Alloy`, `...`

In (Ammicht et al., 2007), the semantic representation of a spoken dialog system is augmented with a dynamic parameter that determines the evolution of a concept-value pair over time, which could be considered as early attempts for coping with user goal changes. However, the determined dynamic confidence score is used to make a hard choice for the candidate semantic values, i.e., determining the birth and death of the observed concept-value pairs. Thomson and Young (2010) introduced a new POMDP-based framework for building spoken dialog systems by using Bayesian updates of dialog state (BUDS). It accommodates for user goal changes by using a dynamic Bayesian network, but BUDS is generative rather than a discriminative model. Therefore it lacks the flexibility of incorporating all kinds of overlapping features – one of the advantages discriminative models have. Furthermore, BUDS assumes limited changes in the user goal in order to gain further efficiency. More recently, Gašić and Young (2011) introduces the explicit representation of complements in partitions which enables negotiation-type dialogs when user goal evolves during the dialog. However, the explicit representation of complements is used to provide existential and universal quantifiers in the system's response.[6] Also a special pruning technique is needed in their approach to ensure the number of partitions doesn't grow exponentially.

Therefore, new approaches for recognizing the event of user goal change and utilizing the goal change information to better infer dialog states have been proposed in the following two subsections 3.2 and 3.3.

3.2 Dialog State Tracking with Detected User Goal Change

Dialog state tracking is usually considered as the core component of a spoken dialog system where dialog manager uses the inferred dialog states to generate system responses (normally through a learned or hand-crafted policy mapping from dialog states to system actions). A specialized version of Maximum Entropy Markov Model with user goal change variable is proposed for dialog state tracking.[7] The most probable dialog state sequence as well as the most likely dialog state value for the latest turn can be inferred given the model. Figure 5 illustrates how the proposed model could infer dialog states of a single concept **Exterior Color** for a dialog of four user turns where the user changes her or his mind at the third dialog turn.[8]

For traditional dialog state tracking methods without user goal change model, the system would be quite confused by completely conflicting observed user actions starting from the third dialog turn. However, the proposed MEMM with user goal change detection could notice that the user has already changed her or his mind. Therefore the proposed model would not only trust more on the observed user actions for the current dialog turn, but also favor those transitions which lead to a different state value by increasing corresponding transition probabilities.

[4]More concepts could also be included such as **Accessories** or **MPG Level**, but only these five concepts are picked for demonstration purpose.

[5]Here *Honda* car models are used as an example.

[6]E.g., "Charlie Chan is the **only** Chinese restaurant in the center." or "**All** Chinese restaurants are in the center."

[7]Methods for detecting user goal change are described in Section 3.3.

[8]We assume every concept in the domain is mutually independent with each other and we model the user goal change separately for each concept.

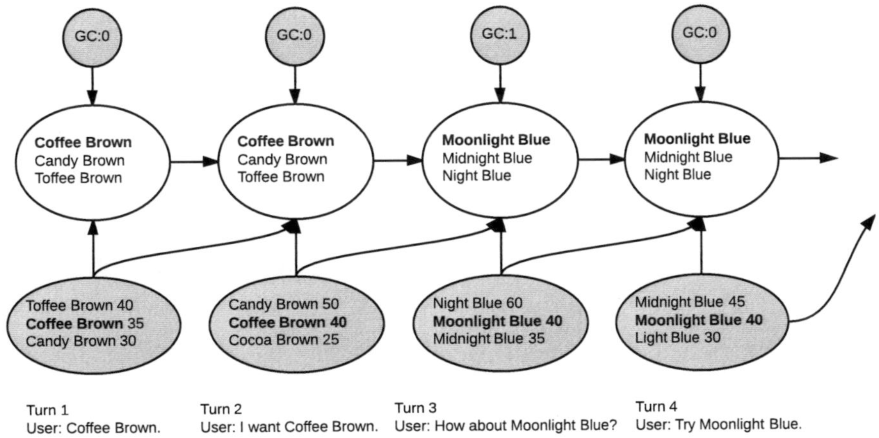

Figure 5: MEMM for dialog state tracking with explicit user goal change variable. A single concept **Exterior Color** from *BuildByVoice* domain is tracked by the model. The shaded nodes are observed user actions and the white nodes are hidden dialog states. The bold text in the observed nodes indicates the true user actions whereas the bold text in the hidden states shows the true dialog state sequence (in this case it is also the most probable decoded dialog state path inferred by the model).

A more formal description of the proposed MEMM is given as follows. The observations o_t (shaded nodes) consist of N-best lists of semantic speech hypotheses (or dialog acts) with confidence scores (scale from 0 to 100) for the current dialog turn hyp_t and previous turn hyp_{t-1} as well as the binary goal change variable gc_t for the current turn – essentially a context window of speech hypotheses including history:

$$o_t = \{hyp_{t-1}, hyp_t, gc_t\}$$

Typically the semantic speech hypotheses hyp_t are extracted concept-value pairs out of ASR results by using a semantic tagger (such as an FST (Finite State Transducer) parser or a segment-based semi-Markov CRF semantic labeler (Liu et al., 2012)). The hidden dialog state q_t (white nodes) represents the user goal for dialog turn t (such as a particular color `Moonlight Blue` for **Exterior Color** at time t). The individual probability of a transition from a state q_{t-1} to a state q_t producing an observation o_t is in a form of the following:

$$P(q_t|q_{t-1}, o_t) = \frac{\exp(\sum_{k=1}^{n} w_k f_k(q_{t-1}, q_t, o_t))}{Z(o_t, q_{t-1})}$$

Given labeled sequences of true dialog states (true user goal) for each turn, the corresponding observations and designed feature functions, we want to learn a set of weights w_k to optimize the discrimination among competing state values given the training data. In other words, the learning procedure involves searching in parameter space to maximize the following conditional likelihood:

$$P(Q|O) = \sum_{i=1}^{N} \prod_{t=1}^{T} \frac{\exp(\sum_{k=1}^{n} w_k f_k(q_{i,t-1}, q_{it}, o_{it}))}{Z(o_{it}, q_{i,t-1})}$$

where N is the number of training dialogs. MEMM can be trained with methods from the field of convex optimization and Viterbi decoding algorithm could be applied to MEMMs for inference (McCallum et al., 2000).

The proposed feature functions are as follows. The first feature function (1a) implies that if the user goal is not changed, the system should look for the common evidence across dialog turns.

$$f(q_t = v, o_t) = \begin{cases} 1 & \text{if } gc_t{=}0 \;\& \\ & v{\in}common(hyp_{t-1}, hyp_t) \\ 0 & \text{otherwise} \end{cases} \tag{1a}$$

where $common(hyp_{t-1}, hyp_t)$ will return the overlapped values from the two N-best lists of dialog acts hyp_{t-1} and hyp_t. The second and third feature functions ((1b) and (1c)) are basically saying that if a user goal change has been detected, then we should expect a different state value, otherwise we should remain the same value from previous dialog turn.

$$f(q_{t-1} = u, q_t = v, o_t) = \begin{cases} 1 & \text{if } gc_t{=}0 \ \& \ u{=}v \\ 0 & \text{otherwise} \end{cases} \tag{1b}$$

$$f(q_{t-1} = u, q_t = v, o_t) = \begin{cases} 1 & \text{if } gc_t{=}1 \ \& \ u{\neq}v \\ 0 & \text{otherwise} \end{cases} \tag{1c}$$

The intuition behind the following four feature functions (feature function (1d) to (1g)) is that if the user changes her or his mind then the model should trust more on the current observed user actions than those from previous turn; but if the user does not change her or his mind, we could then consider the observations from the past.

$$f(q_t = v, o_t) = \begin{cases} 1 & \text{if } gc_t{=}0 \ \& \ v{\in}hyp_{t-1} \\ 0 & \text{otherwise} \end{cases} \tag{1d}$$

$$f(q_t = v, o_t) = \begin{cases} 1 & \text{if } gc_t{=}1 \ \& \ v{\in}hyp_{t-1} \\ 0 & \text{otherwise} \end{cases} \tag{1e}$$

$$f(q_t = v, o_t) = \begin{cases} 1 & \text{if } gc_t{=}0 \ \& \ v{\in}hyp_t \\ 0 & \text{otherwise} \end{cases} \tag{1f}$$

$$f(q_t = v, o_t) = \begin{cases} 1 & \text{if } gc_t{=}1 \ \& \ v{\in}hyp_t \\ 0 & \text{otherwise} \end{cases} \tag{1g}$$

The last two feature functions ((1h) and (1i)) try to incorporate information from confidence scores – the higher the confidence score is, the more likely the hypothesis is to be correct.

$$f(q_t = v, o_t) = \begin{cases} 1 & \text{if } v{\in}hyp_t \ \& \\ & \mathit{confidence}_{hyp_t}(v){>}C \\ 0 & \text{otherwise} \end{cases} \tag{1h}$$

$$f(q_t = v, o_t) = \begin{cases} 1 & \text{if } gc_t{=}0 \ \& \\ & v{\in}hyp_{t-1} \ \& \\ & \mathit{confidence}_{hyp_{t-1}}(v){>}C \\ 0 & \text{otherwise} \end{cases} \tag{1i}$$

where $\mathit{confidence}_{hyp_t}(v)$ returns the confidence score for value v in the speech hypotheses N-best list hyp_t and C is an empirical constant threshold range between 0 to 100 obtained from the training corpus.

3.3 User Goal Change Detection with Linguistic Features and Dialog Context

In previous subsection 3.2, we assume we already know whether or not user changes her or his mind at each dialog turn, whereas this subsection we discuss the possible approaches on how to detect a user goal change. Detecting user goal changes during a dialog could be cast as a binary classification problem where class 0 means no goal change and class 1 indicates user changes her or his mind during a dialog turn. Candidate machine learning algorithms including MLP (Multi-layer Perceptron), SVM (Support Vector Machine) or Logistic Regression could be applied to this binary classification problem in a supervised manner. The input features might be extracted from user utterance transcription[9] and the corresponding ASR N-best list for each dialog turn. As mentioned in Section 2, the language patterns found in the user utterances as presented in the example dialog (shown in Figure 2) forms the intuition for linguistic features to identify user goal change. The dialog context such as last system action could also be included as useful hint for predicting a potential user goal change – user is likely to change her or his goal if system returns empty results for a request. Also other helpful features could include bag of words model, n-grams, prosodic features (e.g., a pitch change or initial pause) and parsed features (e.g., WH questions). Baseline system such as key word spotting based approach (i.e. look for *How/What about* in a sentence) could also be implemented for performance comparison.[10]

4 Conclusion

By modeling the user goal change in a probabilistic framework, the proposed approach should better exploit the mutual information buried deep in the ASR N-best lists across dialog turns, which leads to more robust and accurate dialog state estimation. With the ability to predict and handle user goal change, proposed techniques provide a bottom-up solution for managing negotiation style dialogs and not only should produce more efficient and natural conversations but also open up new possibilities for automated negotiation dialog policy learning.

[9] At test time, this could be approximated by the top hypothesis in the ASR N-best list.

[10] A detailed list of proposed features is omitted due to space limit.

References

Egbert Ammicht, Eric Fosler-Lussier, and Alexandros Potamianos. 2007. Information seeking spoken dialogue systems—part i: Semantics and pragmatics. *Multimedia, IEEE Transactions on*, 9(3):532–549.

M. Gašić and S. Young. 2011. Effective handling of dialogue state in the hidden information state pomdp-based dialogue manager. *ACM Transactions on Speech and Language Processing (TSLP)*, 7(3):4.

James Henderson, Oliver Lemon, and Kallirroi Georgila. 2008. Hybrid reinforcement/supervised learning of dialogue policies from fixed data sets. *Computational Linguistics*, 34(4):487–511.

J. Liu, S. Cyphers, P. Pasupat, I. McGraw, and J. Glass. 2012. A conversational movie search system based on conditional random fields. In *INTERSPEECH*.

A. McCallum, D. Freitag, and F. Pereira. 2000. Maximum entropy markov models for information extraction and segmentation. In *Proceedings of the Seventeenth International Conference on Machine Learning*, volume 951, pages 591–598.

A. Raux and Y. Ma. 2011. Efficient probabilistic tracking of user goal and dialog history for spoken dialog systems. In *Twelfth Annual Conference of the International Speech Communication Association*.

Blaise Thomson and Steve Young. 2010. Bayesian update of dialogue state: A pomdp framework for spoken dialogue systems. *Computer Speech & Language*, 24(4):562–588.

J.D. Williams and S. Young. 2007. Partially observable markov decision processes for spoken dialog systems. *Computer Speech & Language*, 21(2):393–422.

Jason D Williams. 2010. Incremental partition recombination for efficient tracking of multiple dialog states. In *Acoustics Speech and Signal Processing (ICASSP), 2010 IEEE International Conference on*, pages 5382–5385. IEEE.

S. Young, M. Gašić, S. Keizer, F. Mairesse, J. Schatzmann, B. Thomson, and K. Yu. 2010. The hidden information state model: A practical framework for pomdp-based spoken dialogue management. *Computer Speech & Language*, 24(2):150–174.

Author Index

Association for Computational Linguistics
209 N. Eighth Street
Stroudsburg, Pennsylvania 18360

CURRAN ASSOCIATES INC
proceedings.com